METALLICA

AF394438

HAL•LEONARD®

PUBLISHED BY
HAL LEONARD

EXCLUSIVE DISTRIBUTORS:
HAL LEONARD
7777 WEST BLUEMOUND ROAD,
MILWAUKEE, WI 53213
EMAIL: INFO@HALLEONARD.COM

HAL LEONARD EUROPE LIMITED
42 WIGMORE STREET, MARYLEBONE,
LONDON W1U 2RY
EMAIL: INFO@HALLEONARDEUROPE.COM

HAL LEONARD AUSTRALIA PTY. LTD.
4 LENTARA COURT CHELTENHAM,
VICTORIA 9132, AUSTRALIA
EMAIL: INFO@HALLEONARD.COM.AU

ORDER NO. AM91363
ISBN 0-7119-3625-0

WWW.HALLEONARD.COM

METALLICA

LEGEND OF MUSIC SYMBOLS

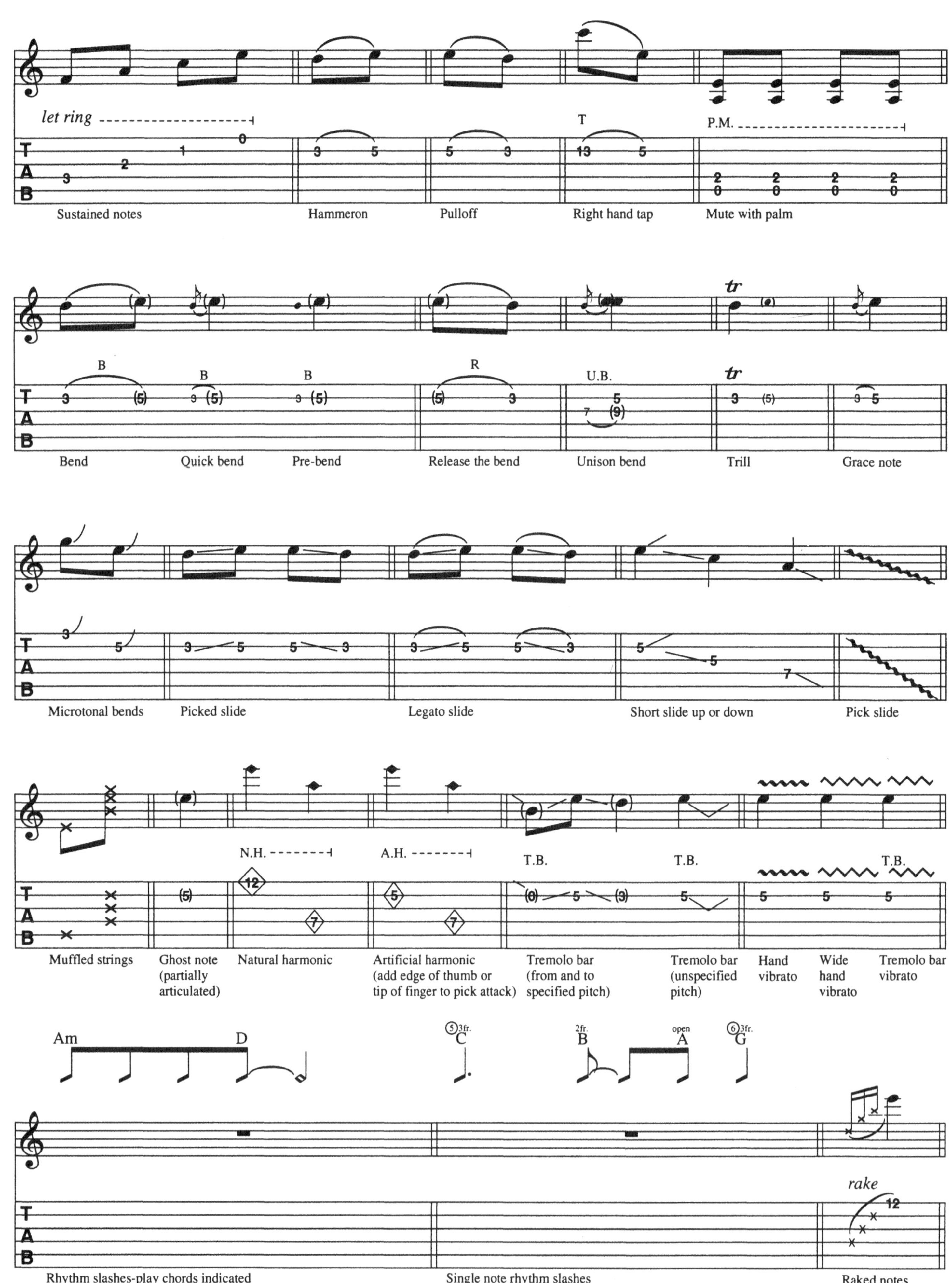

ENTER SANDMAN

WORDS & MUSIC BY JAMES HETFIELD, LARS ULRICH & KIRK HAMMETT

A5
E5
P.M.
play 7 times
(cont. in notation)
guitars 3 & 4
N.C.
E5
Rhythm figure 1
P.M.
N.C.
E5
N.C.
G5
F#5
G5 F#5 E5
P.M.
end Rhythm figure 1
1st, 2nd Verses
N.C.
F5
N.C.
F5
N.C.
G5
1. Say your prayers, lit - tle one. Don't for - get, my son, __ to in - clude ev - 'ry - one.
2. Some-thing's wrong. Shut the light. Heav - y thoughts to - night, __ and they aren't of Snow White.
P.M.

2nd time with Fill 2
F#5   G5 F#5 E5   F5 N.C.   F5
I tuck you in,   warm with - in,   keep you free from   sin __
Dreams of war,   dreams of   li'rs,   dreams of drag - on's   fire __
P.M.   P.M.   P.M.
N.C.   G5   F#5   G5 F#5 N.C.   Half time feel
Pre-chorus
__   till the sand - man, he comes, ________________ ah.
__   and   of things that will bite, ________________ yeah.
Sleep with   one __
Rhythm fill 1
P.M.   P.M.
Rhythm figure 2
(end half time feel)
__ eye   o - pen,   grip-ping your pil - low   tight. ______
P.M.   P.M.   P.M.
end Rhythm figure 2
Fill 2   F#5   G5 F#5   E5   F5
guitar 2
with wah

Chorus
F♯5 B5 F♯5 B5 F♯5 B5 E5
Ex - it: light. ___ En - ter: night. _
Rhythm figure 3
T
A
B
guitar 4 substitutes Rhythm fill 2
guitar 4 substitutes Rhythm fill 3
F♯5 B5 E5
to Coda
G5 F♯5 G5 F♯5 E5
Take ___ my hand. ___ We're off to nev-er-nev-er land. ___
guitar 3
guitars 3 & 4
end Rhythm figure 3
P.M.
with Rhythm figure 1
2nd time with Fill 1
N.C. E5 N.C. E5 N.C. G5
1.
F♯5 G5 F♯5 E5
(Sing 1st time only)
Rhythm fill 2
guitar 4
P.M.
Rhythm fill 3
guitar 4
P.M.
Fill 1
guitar 2
with wah
grad. bend

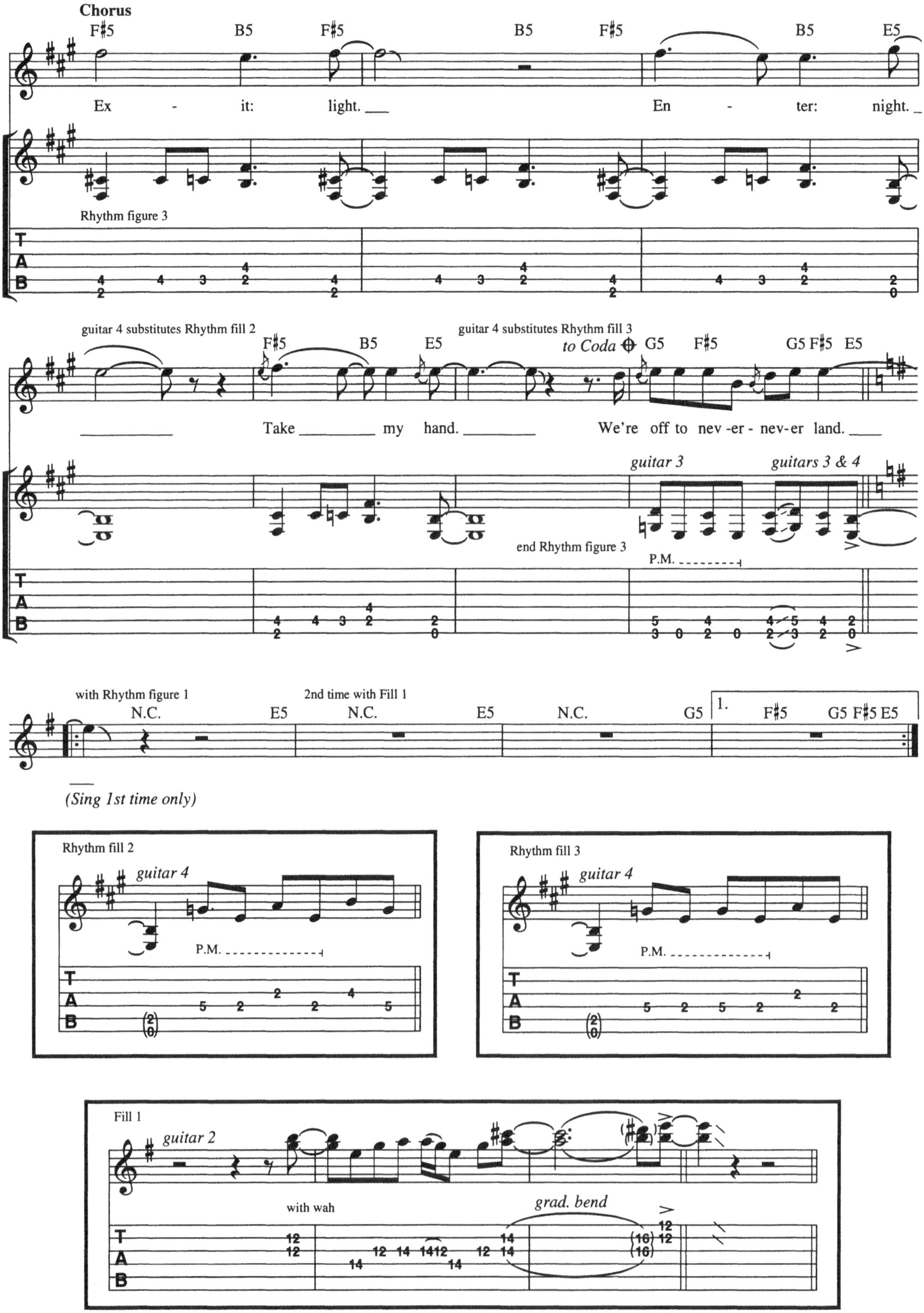

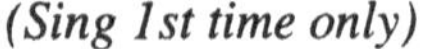

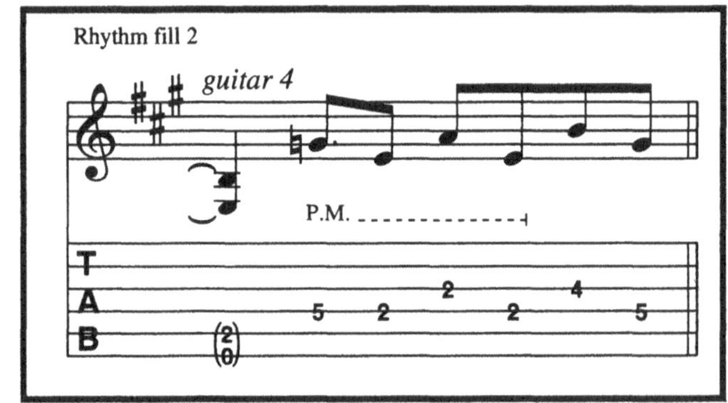

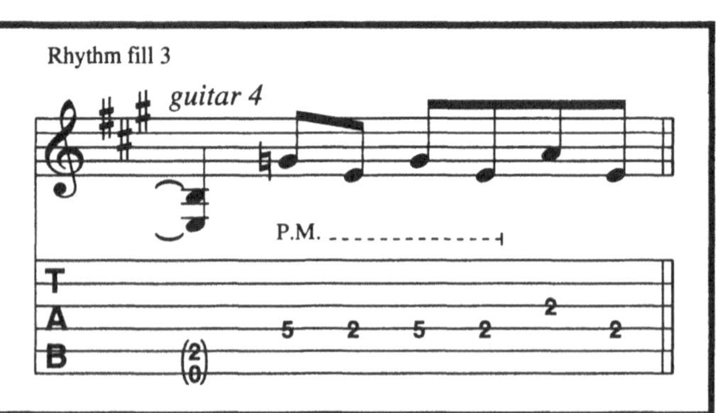

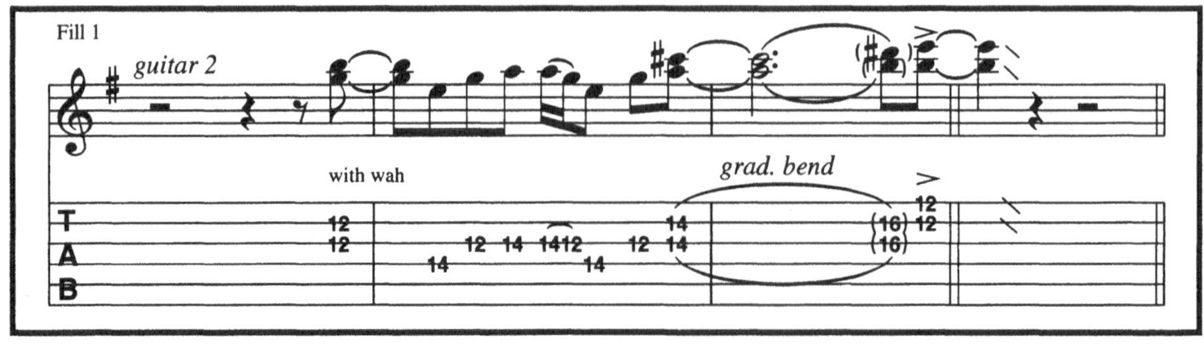

2.
D.S. al Coda
F#5   G5 F#5 E5
Coda
G5   F#5   G5   E5
off to nev-er-nev-er land. ________ Heh, heh
guitar 3
guitars 3 & 4
P.M.
Guitar solo
with Rhythm figure 1 (1¾ times)
N.C.   E5   N.C.   E5   N.C.   G5
guitar 2
with wah
F#5   G5 F#5 E5   N.C.   E5
N.C.   E5   N.C.   G5
8va
with Rhythm fill 1   F#5   G5 F#5 N.C.
Half time feel
with Rhythm figure 2
8va

with Rhythm figure 3
(end half time feel)
F#5   B5   F#5
B5   F#5
B5   E5
F#5
8va
B5   E5
T.B.*
* Gradually release bend and articulate
with tremolo bar simultaneously
E5
8va
guitars 3 & 4
guitar 1
6 open
E
mp
T.B.
T.B.
(Wah off)
T.B.

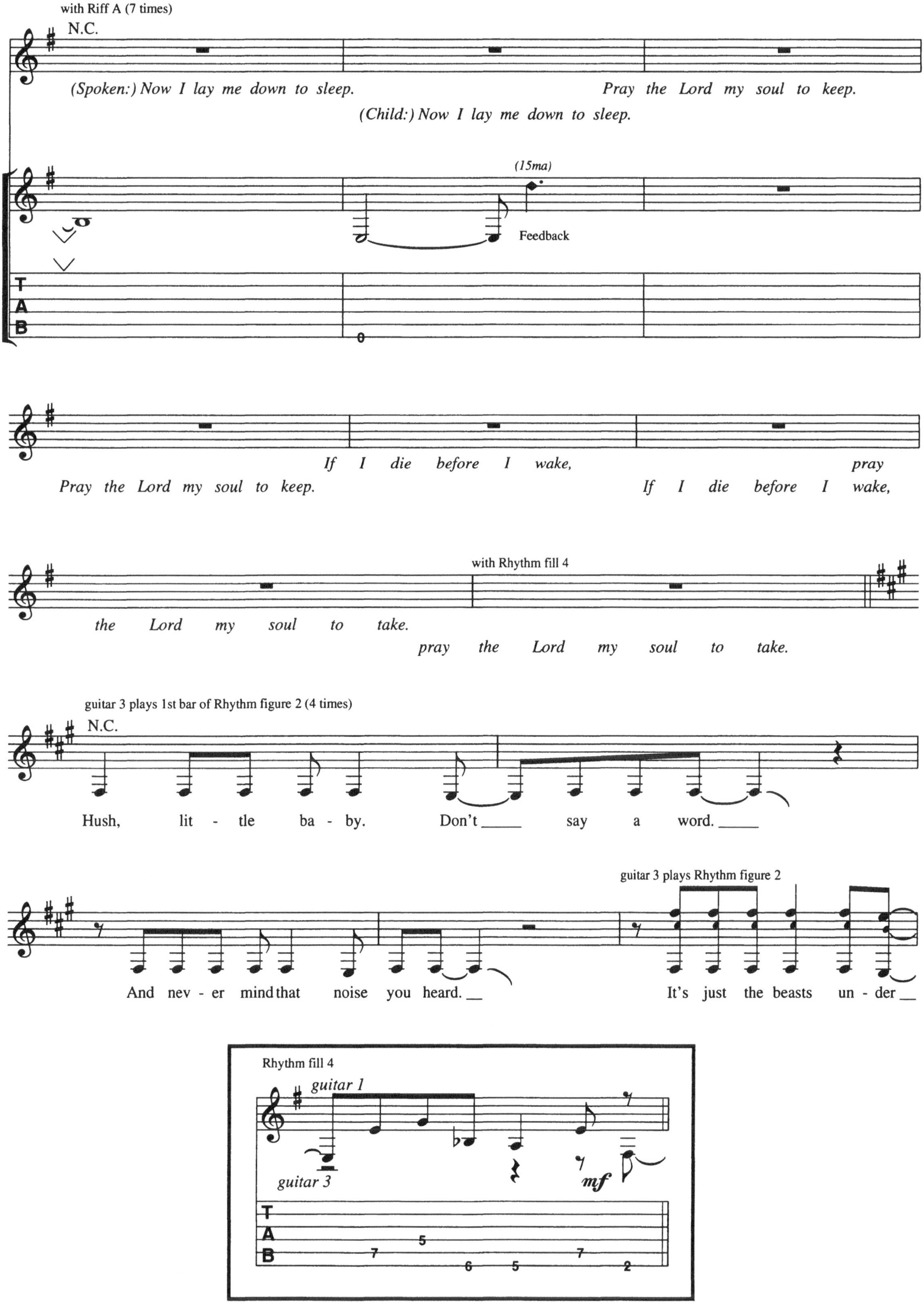

with Riff A (7 times)
N.C.
(Spoken:) Now I lay me down to sleep.
Pray the Lord my soul to keep.
(Child:) Now I lay me down to sleep.
(15ma)
Feedback
Pray the Lord my soul to keep.
If I die before I wake,
pray
If I die before I wake,
the Lord my soul to take.
pray the Lord my soul to take.
guitar 3 plays 1st bar of Rhythm figure 2 (4 times)
N.C.
Hush, lit - tle ba - by. Don't _____ say a word. _____
guitar 3 plays Rhythm figure 2
And nev - er mind that noise you heard. __ It's just the beasts un - der __

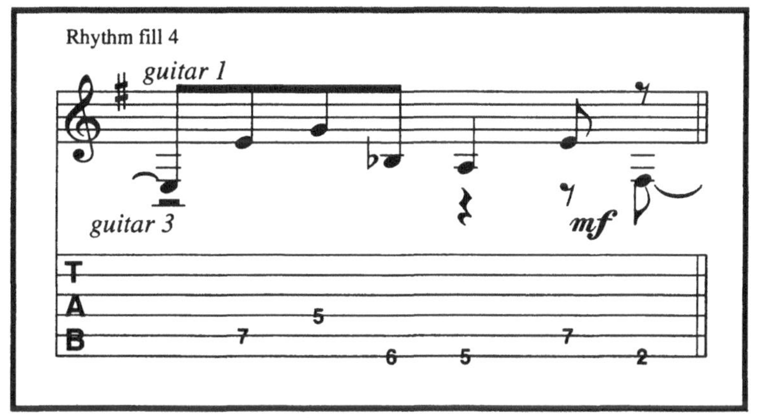
Rhythm fill 4
guitar 1
guitar 3
mf
T
A
B
7
5
6   5
7
2

guitar 4
F#5
P.M.
P.M.
___ your bed ___   in your clos - et,   in ___ your   head. ___________

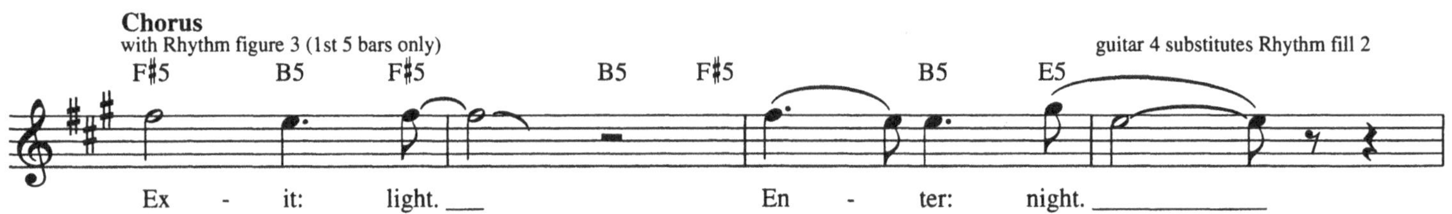

Chorus
with Rhythm figure 3 (1st 5 bars only)
guitar 4 substitutes Rhythm fill 2
F#5   B5   F#5   B5   F#5   B5   E5
Ex - it: light. ___   En - ter: night. ____________

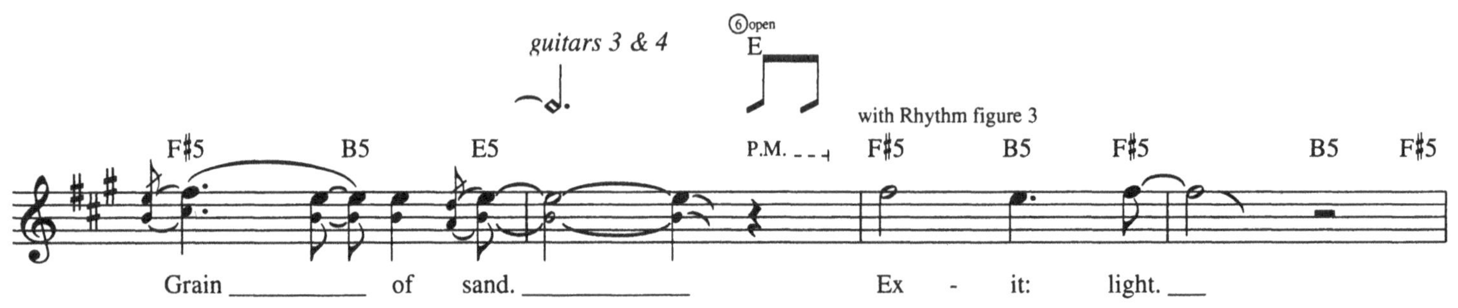

guitars 3 & 4
⑥ open
E
P.M.
with Rhythm figure 3
F#5   B5   E5   F#5   B5   F#5   B5   F#5
Grain _________ of sand. ___________   Ex - it: light. ___

B5   E5   guitar 4 substitutes Rhythm fill 2   F#5   B5   E5   guitar 4 substitutes Rhythm fill 3
En - ter: night. ____________   Take _______ my hand. ___________   We're

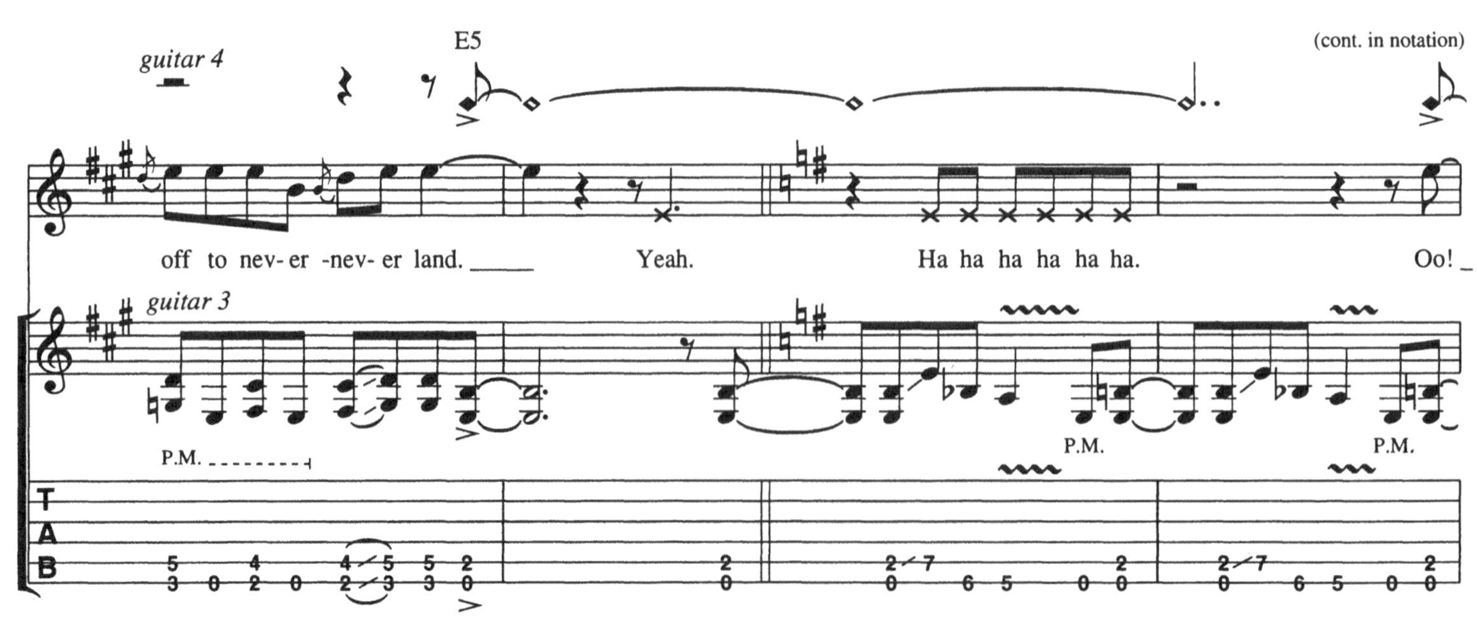

guitar 4
E5
(cont. in notation)
off to nev- er -nev- er land. ___   Yeah.   Ha ha ha ha ha ha.   Oo! _
guitar 3
P.M.
P.M.
P.M.
T
A
B
5 4   4 5 5 2
3 0   2 3 3 0
2
0
2 7   2
0 6 5 0 0
2 7   2
0 6 5 0 0

N.C.
E5
N.C.
E5
N.C.
E5
guitars 3 & 4
P.M.
Yeah, __ yeah! _________________
N.C.
E5
N.C.
guitar 1
G5
⑥open
E
p
P.M.
Yo, _________ woh!
with Riff A (till end)
N.C.
F5
N.C.
F5
N.C.
F5
P.M.
with vocal ad lib (till end)
N.C.
F5
N.C.
F5
N.C.
Play 4 times
5th time with Fill 3
Repeat and fade
P.M.
Fill 3
guitar 2
N.C.
mp
3
3
(Wah off)

SAD BUT TRUE

WORDS & MUSIC BY JAMES HETFIELD LARS ULRICH

Tune down one whole step:
6 = D 3 = F
5 = G 2 = A
4 = C 1 = D
D5
Bb5
Moderately slow ♩ = 86
Intro
Gtr. 1
A5
Bb5
A5
N.C.
f
P.M.
1.
(Bb5)
2.
F5
N.C.
E5
N.C.
E5
N.C.
E5
N.C.
P.M.
P.M.
P.M.
1.
E5
N.C.
2.
E5
N.C.
P.M.
P.M.

E5   N.C.   E5   N.C.   (cont. in slashes)
P.M.
B   R
P.M.

1st, 2nd, 3rd Verses
⑥   ⑥open   ⑥open
E   D5 E   Bb5   E   end Rhythm figure 1
Rhythm figure 1
P.M.   P.M.   P.M.   P.M.   P.M.

1.Hey,   I'm your life.   I'm the one who takes you there. ___
2.You,   you're my mask.   You're my cov - er, my shel - ter. ___
3. Hate,   I'm your hate.   I'm your hate when you want love. ___

with Rhythm figure 1 (3 times)   ⑥open
3rd time substitute Rhythm fill 1
D5 E   Bb5   ⑥open E   ⑥open D5 E

Hey, __   I'm your life.   I'm the one who cares. ___   They, ____   they be - tray.
You, __   you're my mask.   You're the one who's blamed. __   Do, _____   do my work.
Pay, ___   pay the price.   Pay, for noth-ing's fair. ____   Hey, ____   I'm your life.

Bb5   ⑥open E   ⑥open D5 E   Bb5   ⑥open E

I'm your on - ly true friend now.   They, __   they'll be - tray.   I'm for - ev - er there. ____
Do my dirt - y work, scape- goat.   Do, ___   do my deeds, for you're the one who's shamed. ___
I'm the one who took you there.   Hey, ___   I'm your life. And I no long - er care. ____

Chorus
N.C.   F5   D5 F5   F5   D5   N.C. A5

I'm your dream, _   make you real. ___   I'm your eyes _ when you must

P.M.   Rhythm figure 2   P.M.   P.M.

Rhythm fill 1
⑥open
E   Bb5   ⑥open E Bb5   ⑥open E Bb5
P.M.   P.M.   P.M.

to Coda
Bb5 G5   A5 G5   C5   N.C. F5 N.C.
steal. I'm your pain __ when you can't feel.   Sad but true. _______
P.M.
P.M.
end Rhythm figure 2
F5   D5 F5 E5   F5   D5 N.C. A5
__ I'm your dream, __ mind a-stray. ___   I'm your eyes __ when you're a-
P.M.
P.M.
P.M.
Bb5 G5   A5 G5   C5   N.C. F5 N.C.
way. I'm your pain __ while you re-pay. _______   You know it's sad but true. _______
P.M.
P.M.
E5   N.C.   E5   N.C.   1. E5   N.C.
__   Sad __ but   true. ____________
P.M.
P.M.
P.M.

E5
N.C.
P.M.
E5
N.C.
E5
N.C.
P.M.
P.M.
2.
E5
N.C.
true.
P.M.
Interlude
A5
guitar 2
Bb5
A5
guitar 1
P.M.
P.M.
Bb5
A5
Bb5
P.M.
P.M.

A5
Bb5
N.C.
P.M.
Guitar solo I
E5
N.C.
E5
N.C.
P.M.
P.M.
E5
N.C.
E5
N.C.
P.M.
P.M.
18

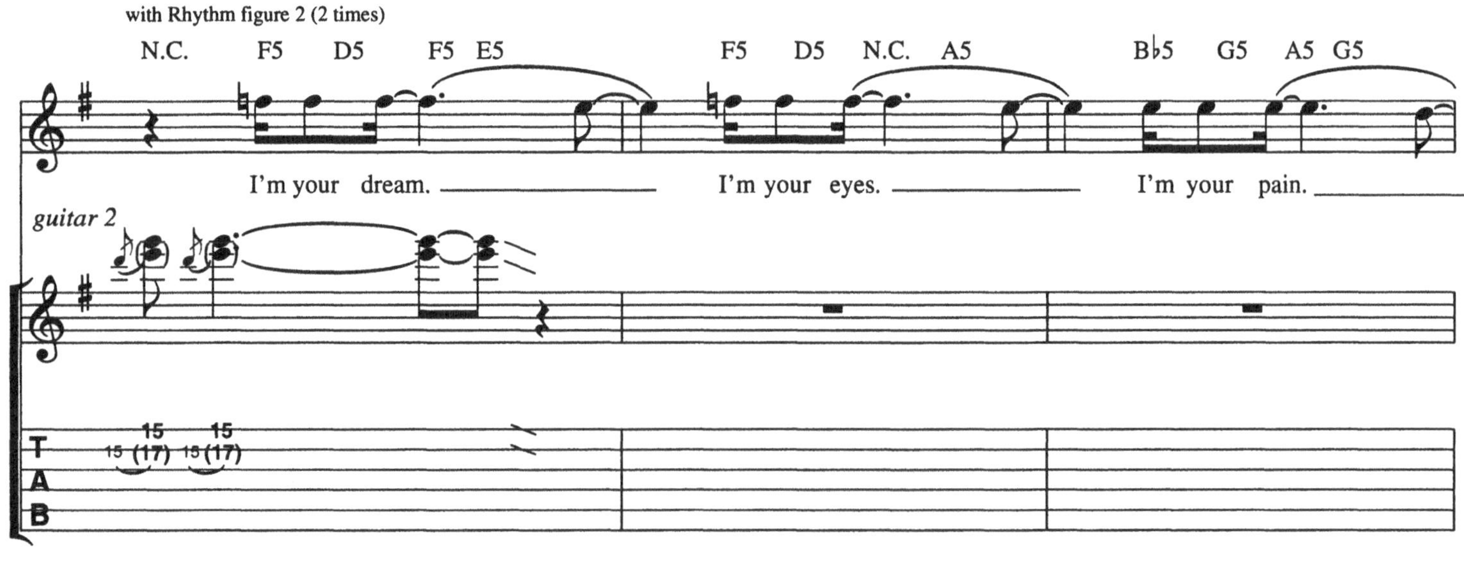

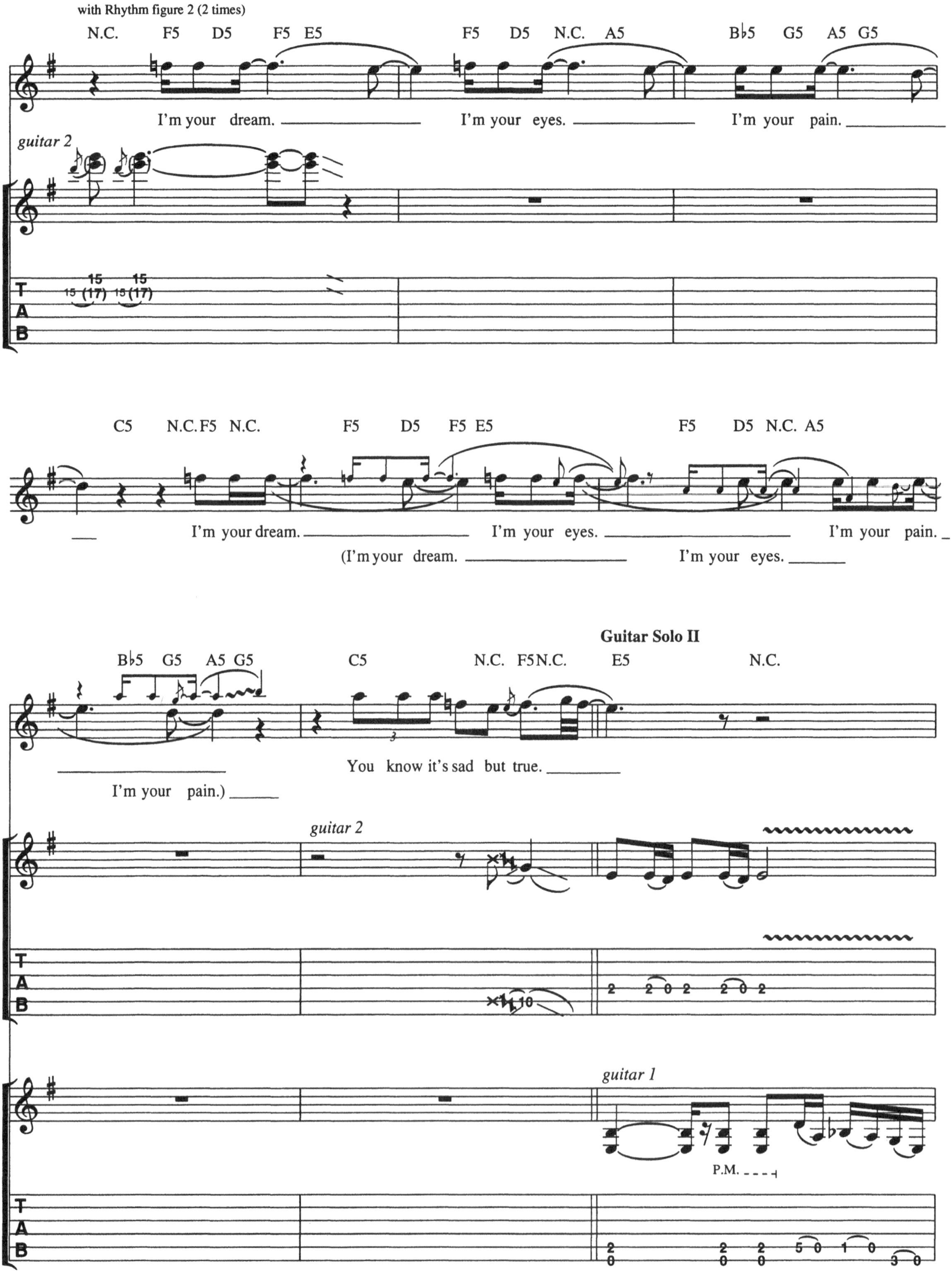
with Rhythm figure 2 (2 times)
N.C. F5 D5 F5 E5 F5 D5 N.C. A5 B♭5 G5 A5 G5
I'm your dream. I'm your eyes. I'm your pain.
guitar 2
C5 N.C. F5 N.C. F5 D5 F5 E5 F5 D5 N.C. A5
I'm your dream. I'm your eyes. I'm your pain.
(I'm your dream. I'm your eyes.
Guitar Solo II
B♭5 G5 A5 G5 C5 N.C. F5 N.C. E5 N.C.
You know it's sad but true.
I'm your pain.)
guitar 2
guitar 1
P.M.

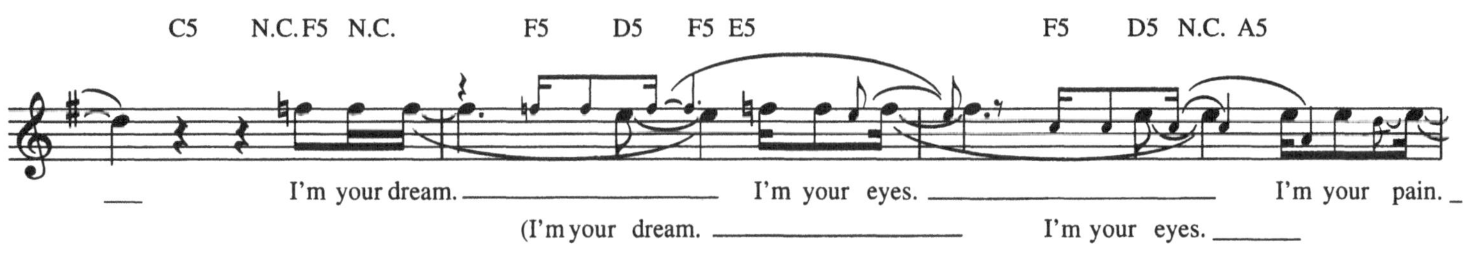

E5
N.C
E5
N.C
(semi-harmonics)
P.M.
E5
N.C
E5
N.C
P.M.
P.M.
guitar 1
D.S. al Coda
21

Coda
with Rhythm figure 2
F5   D5   F5   E5   F5   D5   N.C. A5
___   I'm your   truth, ___   tell - ing   lies. ___   I'm your   rea - son,   al - i -

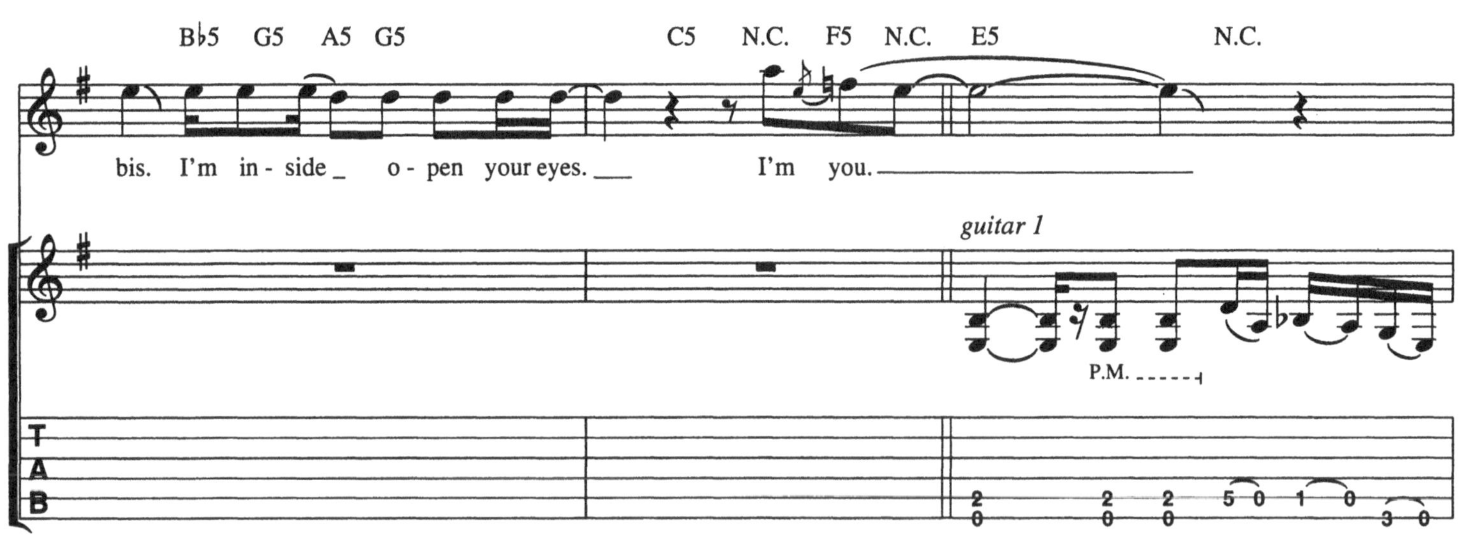

Bb5 G5 A5 G5   C5 N.C. F5 N.C. E5   N.C.
bis. I'm   in - side _   o - pen   your eyes. ___   I'm   you. ___
guitar 1
P.M.
2   2 2 5 0 1 0
0   0 0   3 0

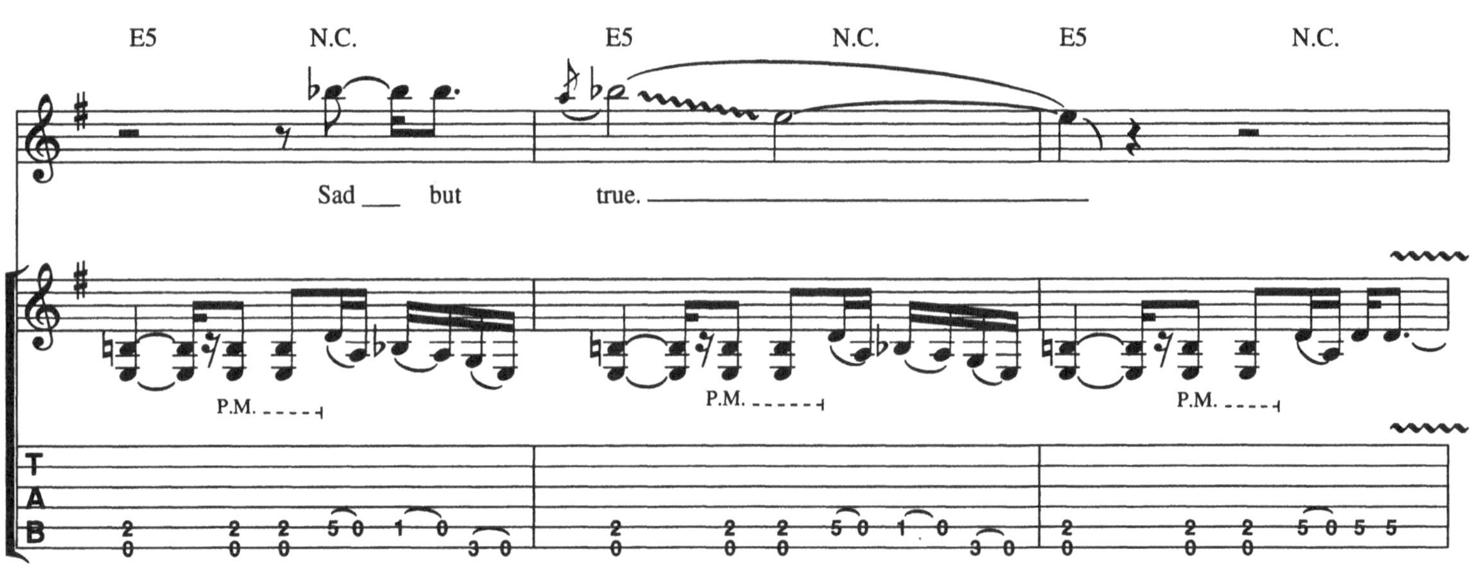

E5   N.C.   E5   N.C.   E5   N.C.
Sad ___ but   true. ___
P.M.   P.M.   P.M.
2   2 2 5 0 1 0   2   2 2 5 0 1 0   2   2 2 5 0 5 5
0   0 0   3 0   0   0 0   3 0   0   0 0

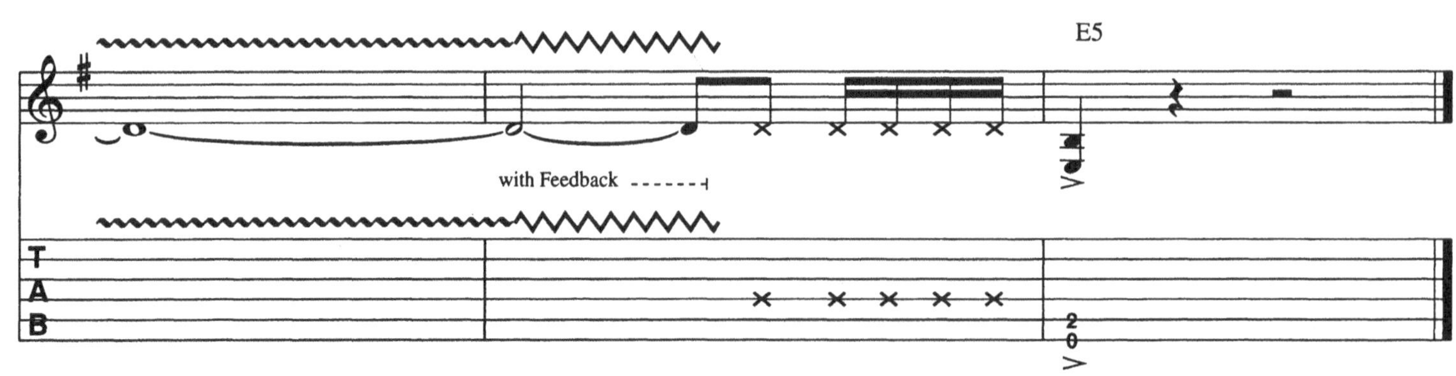

E5
with Feedback
2
0

HOLIER THAN THOU

WORDS & MUSIC BY JAMES HETFIELD LARS ULRICH

N.C.
E5
N.C.
E5
N.C.
P.M.

E5
N.C.
E5
N.C.
E5
P.M.
Rhythm fill 1

1st Verse

N.C.
G5
N.C.
E5
No more! The crap rolls out your mouth a - gain.
(end Rhy. Fill 1)
P.M.
Rhythm figure 2
P.M.
end Rhythm fill 1

N.C.
G5
N.C.
E5
Have - n't changed, your brain __ is still gel - a - tin. Lit - tle whis-pers cir - cle a - round _ your head.
P.M.
P.M.

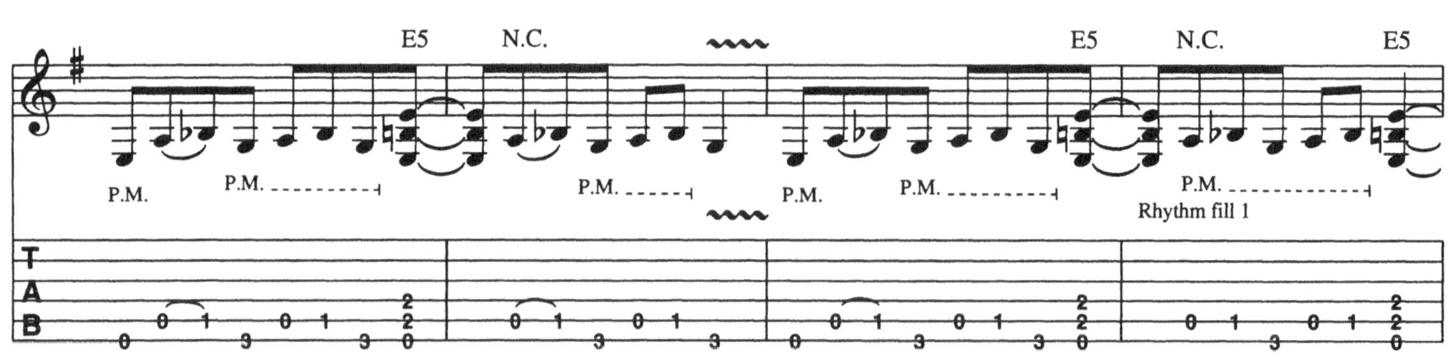

N.C.
E5
Why don't you wor - ry a - bout ____ your - self ____ in - stead? ____
P.M.
end Rhythm figure 2
N.C.
G5
with Rhythm figure 2
Who are you? _Where
P.M.
P.M.
P.M.
Rhythm fill 2
end Rhythm fill 2
N.C.
E5
N.C.
G5
___ ya been? Where ya from? Gos - sip burn - ing on ____ the tip of ___ your tongue. You lie so much_
N.C.
E5
N.C.
E5
___ you be - lieve __ your - self. Judge not lest ye ____ be judged _ your - self. ____
Chorus
N.C.
E5
N.C.
E5
N.C.
E5
Ho - li - er than __ thou, ____ you are. _
P.M.
P.M.
P.M.
P.M.
P.M.

N.C.   E5   N.C.   E5   N.C.   E5
Ho - li - er than ___ thou, ___________ you are. __
P.M.   P.M.   P.M.   P.M.
with Rhythm figure 1 (3 times)
to Coda
with Rhythm fill 1
N.C.   E5
You ___ know ___________ not. ___
2nd Verse
N.C.   G5
with Rhythm figure 2
N.C.   E5
Be - fore you judge ___ me take a look at you.   Can't you find some -
N.C.   G5   N.C.   E5
thing bet - ter ___ to do?   Point the fin - ger, slow ___ to un - der - stand. ___
N.C.   E5
___ Ar - ro - gance and ig - nor - ance go ___ hand in hand. ___________
guitar 3
with wah   gradual bend
B
with Rhythm fill 2
R
N.C.   G5

with Rhythm figure 2
N.C.
E5
It's not who you are, ___ it's who __ you know. Oth - ers lives are the ba -
N.C.
G5
N.C.
E5
sis of ___ your own. Burn your bridg - es and build ___ them back ___ with wealth. ___
Feedback
B R B R
D. S. al Coda
N.C.
Judge not, lest ye ___ be judged __ your - self. ___
Coda
N.C.
E5
G5
F#5
F5
E5
Yeah! ___ Who the hell are you? _
guitars 1 & 2
P.M.
P.M.

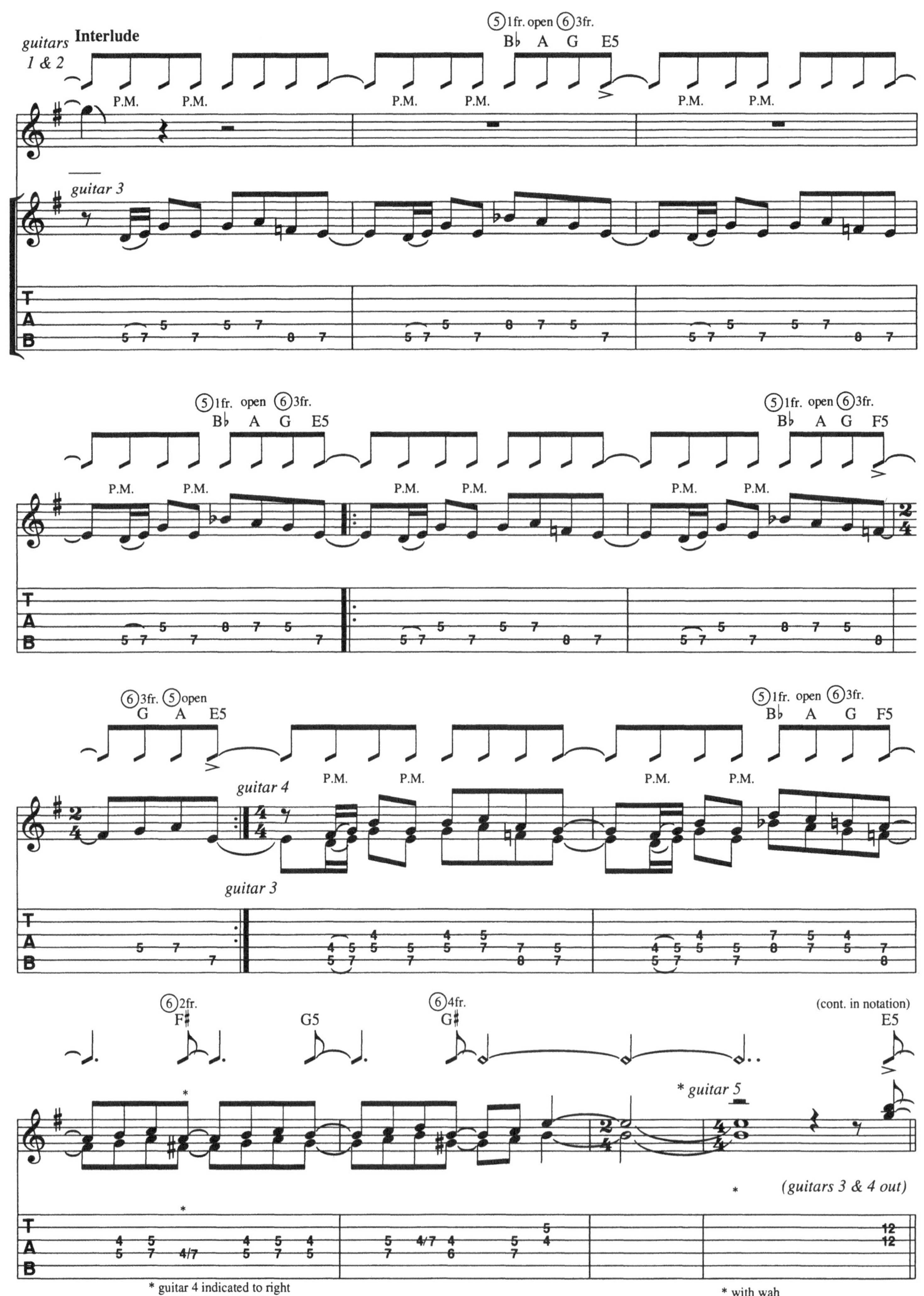

guitars 1 & 2
Interlude
P.M.
guitar 3
5 1fr. open 6 3fr.
B♭ A G E5
5 1fr. open 6 3fr.
B♭ A G E5
5 1fr. open 6 3fr.
B♭ A G F5
6 3fr. 5 open
G A E5
guitar 4
guitar 3
5 1fr. open 6 3fr.
B♭ A G F5
6 2fr.
F#
G5
6 4fr.
G#
(cont. in notation)
E5
* guitar 5
* (guitars 3 & 4 out)
* guitar 4 indicated to right
of slashes in TAB
* with wah

Guitar solo
guitar 5
29

8va
Outro
E5 N.C.
P.M.
P.M.
3
N.C.
guitar 1
E5
N.C.
P.M.
guitars 1 & 2
E5
N.C.
guitars 1, 2, and 3
E5
P.M.

N.C.
E5
N.C.
E5
Ho - li - er than ____ thou, ____________________ you are. _
P.M.
P.M.
P.M.
P.M.

N.C.
E5
N.C.
E5
N.C.
E5
Ho - li - er than ___ thou, ________________ you are _
P.M.
P.M.
P.M.
P.M.

N.C.
E5
You ____ know ____________ not. ____
P.M.
P.M.
P.M.
P.M.

N.C.
G5
N.C.
E5
Woh, ______________ not!
P.M.

THE UNFORGIVEN

WORDS & MUSIC BY JAMES HETFIELD, LARS ULRICH & KIRK HAMMETT

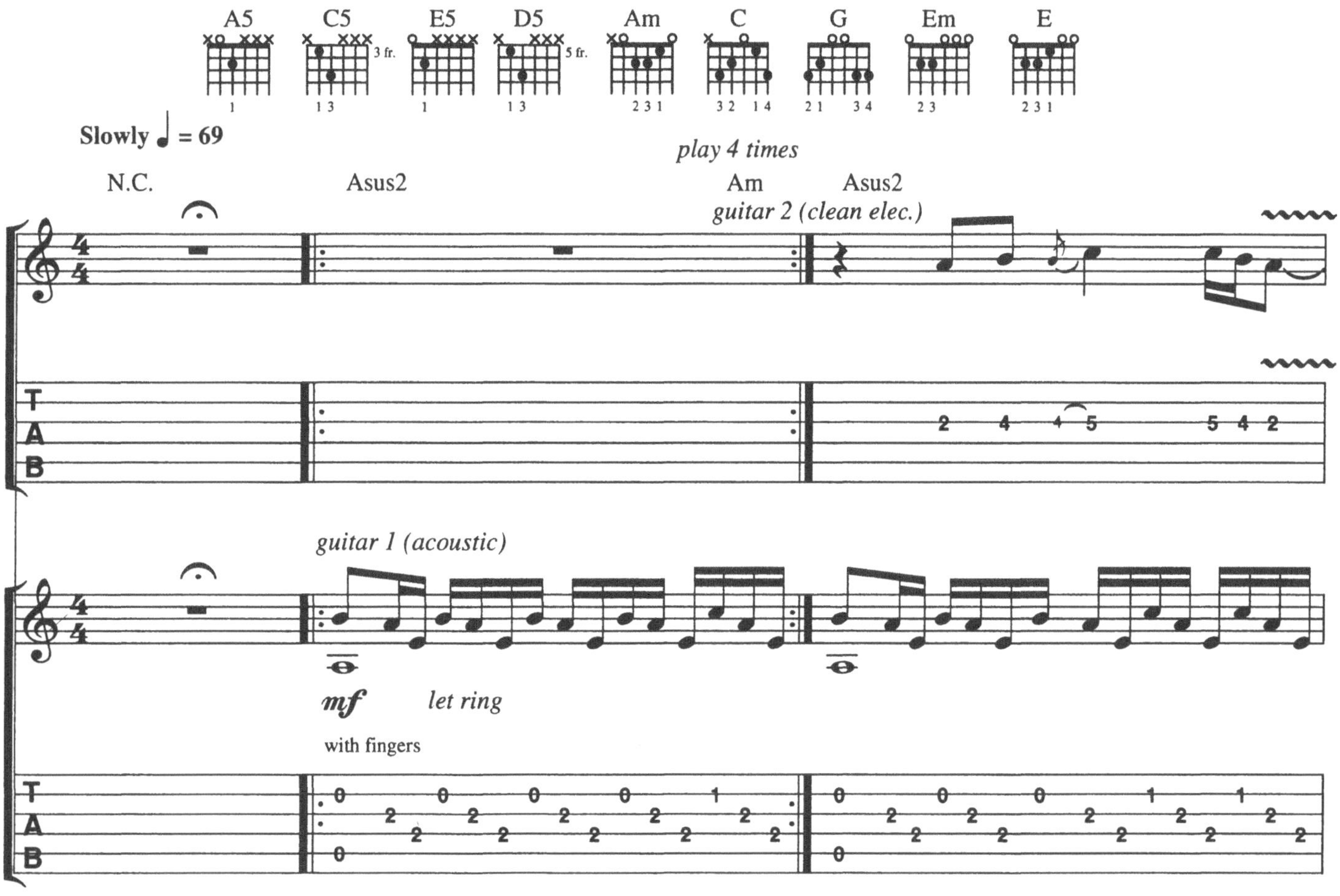

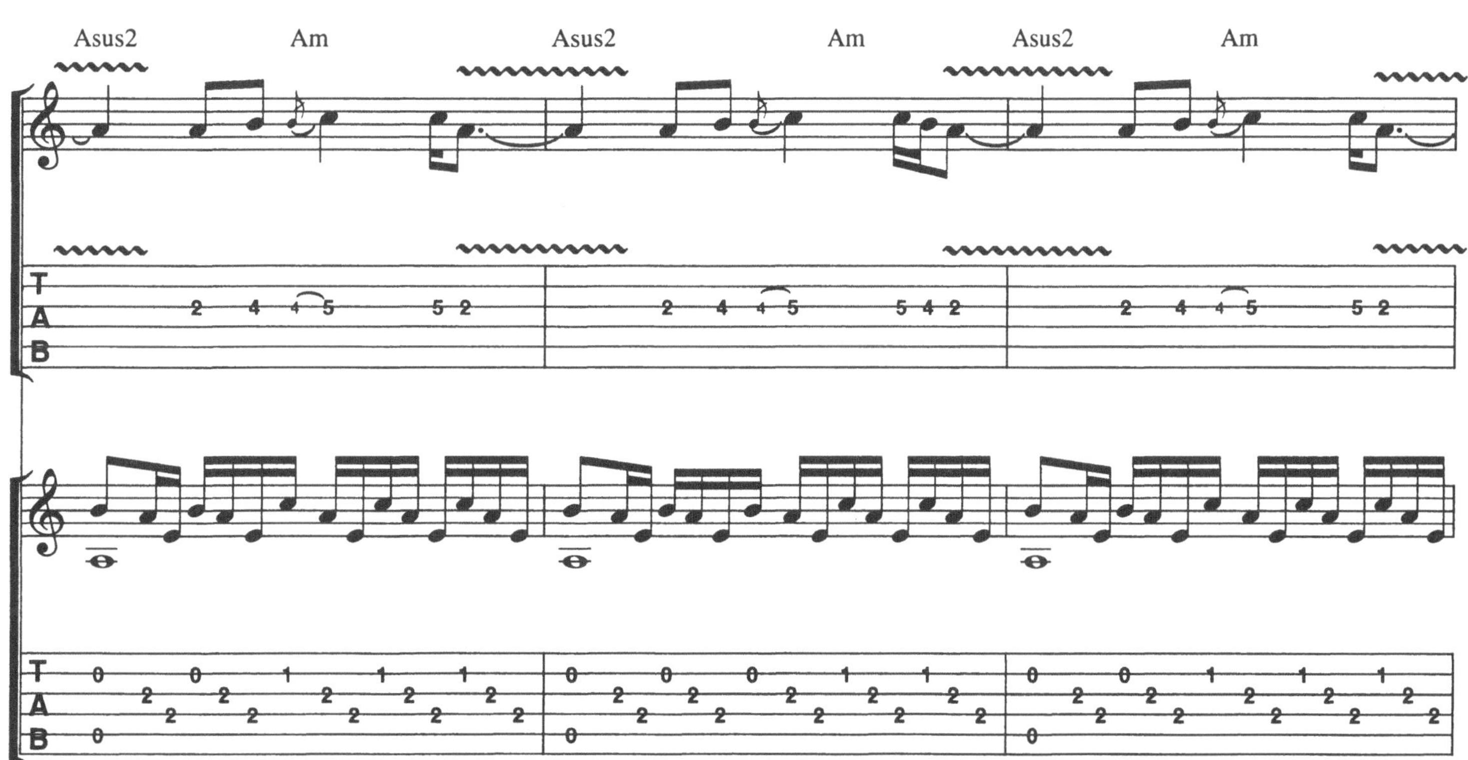

33

Asus2   C   G   E5   Asus2   C
Rhythm figure 1
G   E   Asus2   Am   Asus2   Am
dim.
end Rhythm figure 1
Rhythm figure 2
end Rhythm figure 2
1st, 2nd Verses
end Rhythm figure 3
with Rhythm figure 3 & Riff A (2 times)
⑥open
A5   C5   E5   ⑥open E   D5   A5   A   A5   C5   E5   ⑥open E   D5
Rhythm figure 3
guitar 3
f
P.M.
P.M.
1.New blood _ joins this earth, and quick-ly he's sub-dued. Through con-stant pain _ dis-grace, _ the young _
2. See additional lyrics
guitar 4
f Riff A
end Riff A

A5 A A5 C5 E5 E D5 A5 A A5
boy learns their rules. With time, the child draws in this whip-ping boy done wrong. De-

guitar 3
C5 E5 E D5 (cont. in notation) A5 N.C.
P.M.
prived of all his thoughts, the young man strug-gles on and on. He's known, oo, a

guitar 4
guitar 3
P.M. P.M. P.M. P.M.
Rhythm figure 4

C5 G5 N.C. C5 G5 E5
vow un-to his own that nev-er from this day his will they'll take a-way.
P.M. P.M. P.M. P.M.
(cont. in slashes)
end Rhythm figure 4

Chorus
with Rhythm figure 1 (2 times)
guitar 3
A5 G E5 Asus2 C
What I've felt, what I've known nev-er shined through in what I've shown. Nev-er be Nev-er see.
guitar 2
mf

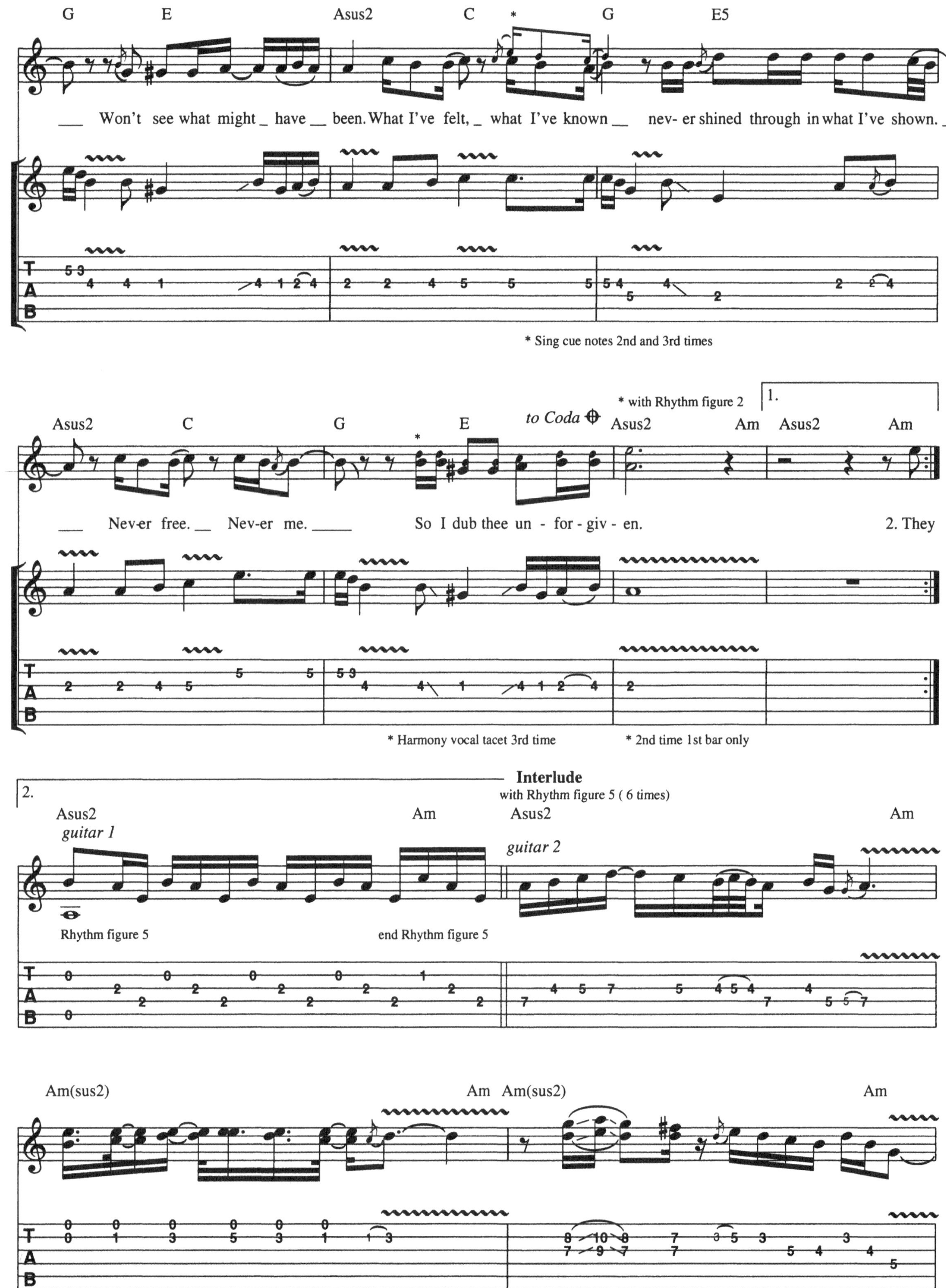

Won't see what might _ have _ been. What I've felt, _ what I've known _ nev- er shined through in what I've shown. _

* Sing cue notes 2nd and 3rd times

* with Rhythm figure 2

to Coda

Nev-er free. _ Nev-er me. _ So I dub thee un - for - giv - en.

* Harmony vocal tacet 3rd time

* 2nd time 1st bar only

2. They

Interlude
with Rhythm figure 5 (6 times)

guitar 1

guitar 2

Rhythm figure 5

end Rhythm figure 5

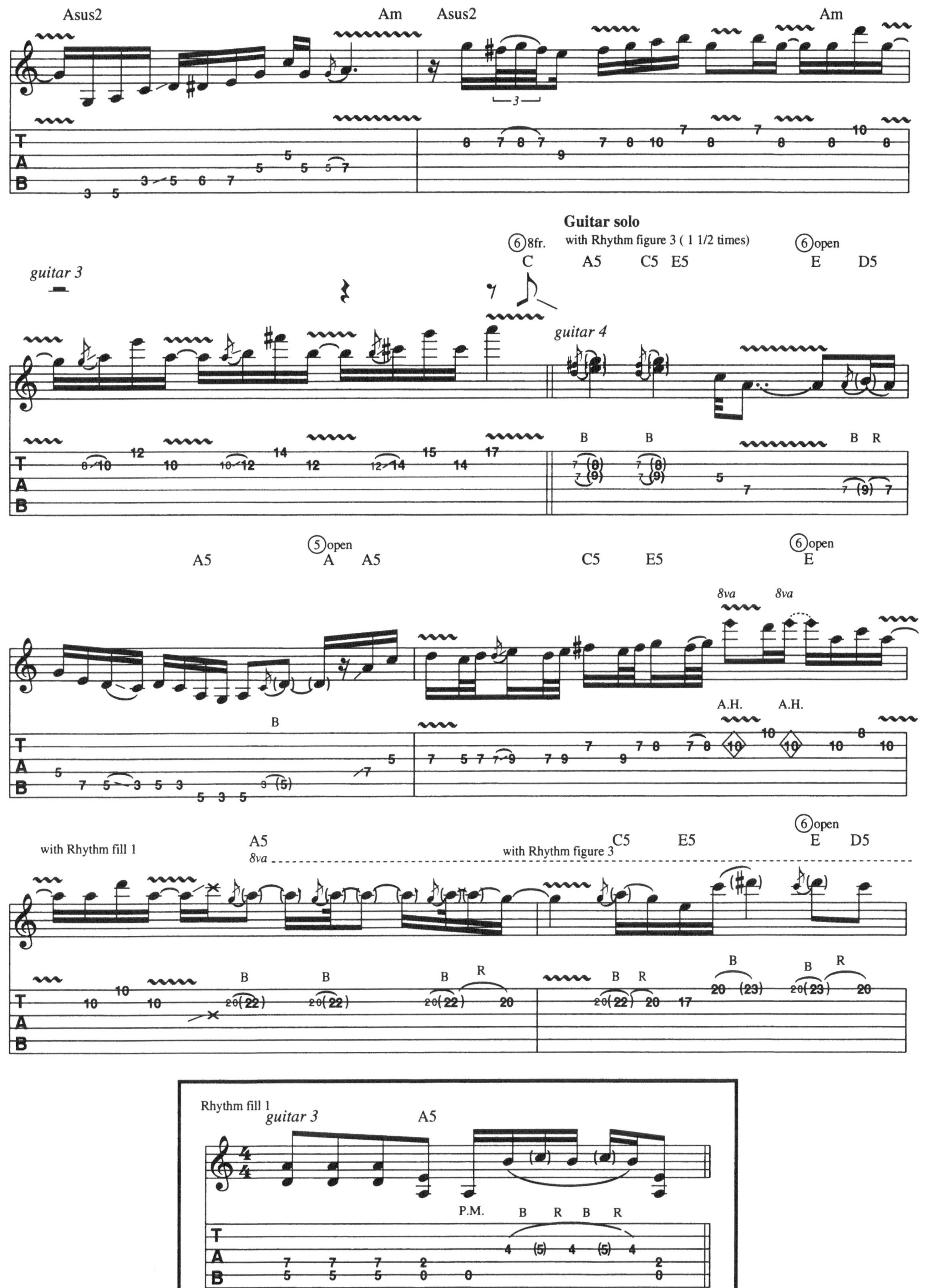

Asus2
Am
Asus2
Am
Guitar solo
with Rhythm figure 3 (1 1/2 times)
guitar 3
guitar 4
C
A5 C5 E5
E D5
8fr.
open
A5
A A5
C5 E5
E
open
open
open
8va 8va
A.H. A.H.
with Rhythm fill 1
A5
C5 E5
E D5
with Rhythm figure 3
8va
open
Rhythm fill 1
guitar 3
A5
P.M.

A5
(5) open
A   A5
guitar 3
C5   E5
(6) open
E   D5
P.M.
8
2/4
B R
(20) 23 20 17 17 2017 17
20
B
20(22)
17
9
10 9 7 9   7
10 8 7   7
9   9 7 5 7 5 4 5 4 2   14

with Rhythm figure 4
A5   N.C.   C5   G5
8va
2/4   4/4
12 13 12 13 12
13 13 13 13 13 13
14   14   14   14   14   14
13 12 13 12 13 12 13 12 13 12
14 14 14 14 14 14
B   B R   B   B
20(22)   20(22)   17 19
19(21) 19(21)(19) 17

N.C.   C5   G5
8va
2/4
3
20 19 17 19 17 19 17   17
20(22)   2017   2017
19(21)   19   19(21) 19 17   19(21) 19 17   19(21)   19(21)19 17
B   B   B R   B R   B   B R
20   18 20 18

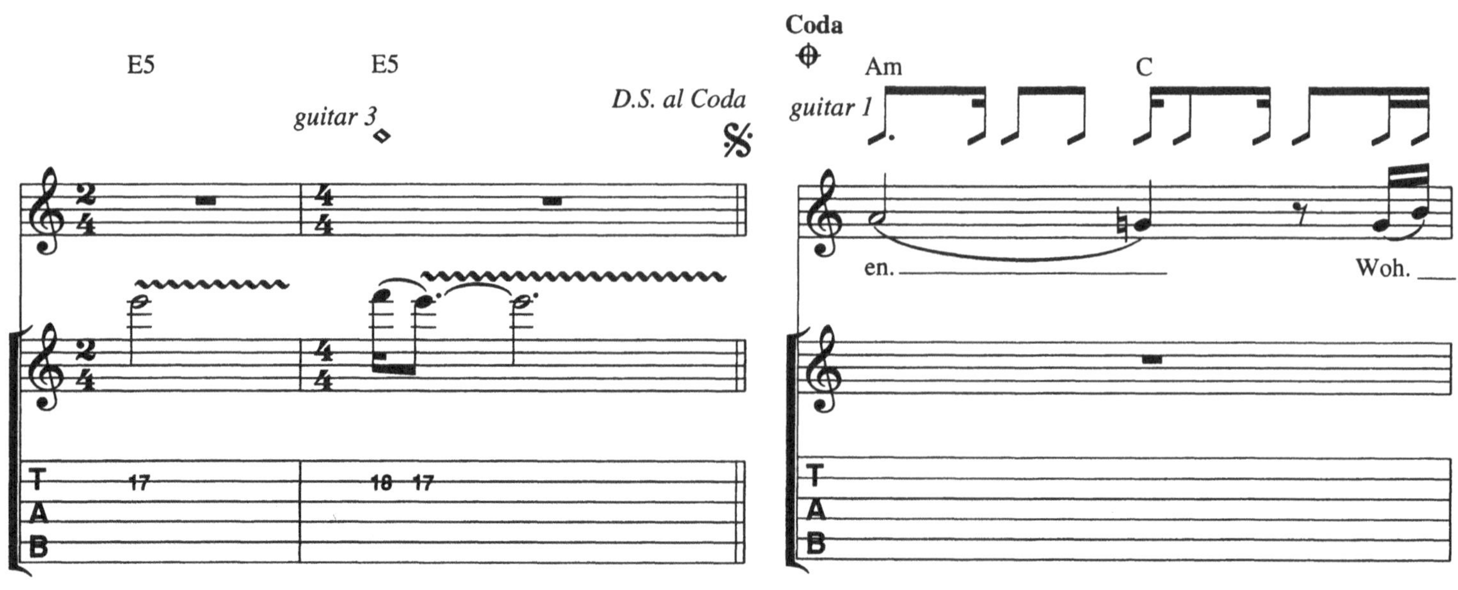
E5   E5
guitar 3
D.S. al Coda
2/4   4/4
17   18 17

Coda
Am   C
guitar 1
en.   Woh.

G   Em   Am   C   G   E
(cont. in Fill1)
guitar 3
guitar 4
guitar 3
both gtrs. vib.
* guitar 4 indicated to left of slash
Outro
1st time with Fill 1
Rhythm figure 6
Am   C   G   E   end Rhythm figure 6
Nev-er free. __ Nev-er me. _______ So I dub thee un-for-giv-
* guitar 2
* 1st time enter on beat 2
with Rhythm figure 6 (3 times) & Riff B
Am   C   G   E   Am   C
en. _________________________ You la-beled me. __ I'll la-bel you. __
Fill 1   Am   C
guitar 4
guitar 3

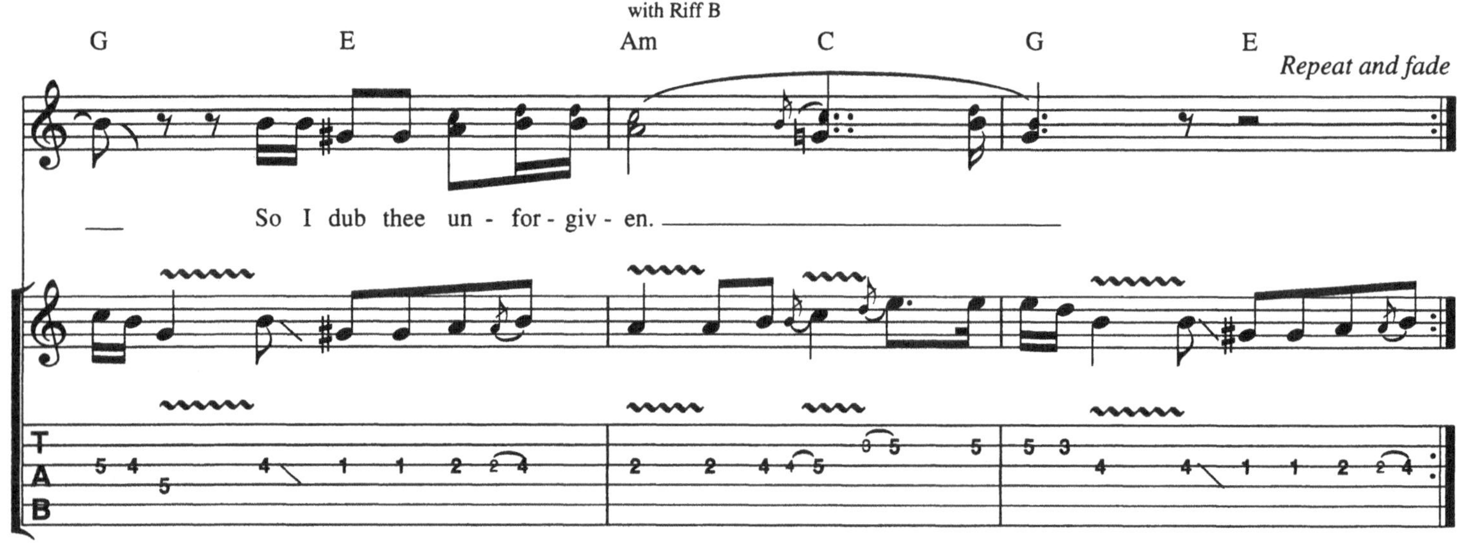

Additional lyrics

2. They dedicate their lives to running all of his.

   He tries to please them all, this bitter man he is.

   Throughout his life the same, he's battled constantly.

   This fight he cannot win. A tired man they see no longer cares.

   The old man then prepares to die regretfully.

   That old man here is me.   *(to Chorus)*

WHEREVER I MAY ROAM
WORDS & MUSIC BY JAMES HETFIELD LARS ULRICH
E5 Bb5 A5 G5 D5 C5 B5 Bb5(type2)
3 fr. 10 fr. 3 fr.
Moderate Rock ♩ = 128
Half time feel
Intro
*guitar 1
mf let ring throughout
* Sitar arranged for guitar
guitar 2 (electric)
5 fr. 20 fr.
A C E5
guitar 3 (electric)
1.
2.
(end half time feel)
A5 A#5 B5 C5
guitars 2 & 3
© COPYRIGHT 1991 CREEPING DEATH MUSIC, USA.
POLYGRAM MUSIC PUBLISHING LIMITED, 1 SUSSEX PLACE, LONDON W6.
ALL RIGHTS RESERVED. INTERNATIONAL COPYRIGHT SECURED.
41

E5 N.C.
E5 N.C.
A5 A#5 B5 C5
tr
tr
Rhythm figure 1
P.M.
P.M.
P.M.
end Rhythm figure 1
N.C.
E5 N.C.
A5 A#5 B5 C5
tr
tr
Rhythm figure 2
P.M.
P.M.
P.M.
end Rhythm figure 2
Half time feel
N.C.
E5
F5
P.M.
P.M.
Em
F5
(Whispered:) And the road be- comes _ my bride. _________
1. And the road be- comes _ my bride. _
(cont. in slashes)
P.M.
P.M.
1st, 2nd Verses
E5
Bb5
_________ I have stripped of all __ but pride, so in her I do __ con -
2. See additional lyrics

42

A5
Bb5
6 open E
P.M.
fide, ______ and she keeps me sat - is - fied. __________ Gives me all I need.
E5
Rhythm figure 3
Bb5
And with dust in throat I crave, ___ on - ly knowl- edge will __ I save _
guitar 4 (clean elec.)
let ring
let ring
G5
Bb5
end half time feel
end Rhythm figure 3
(cont. in notation)
To the game you stay a slave. ___________ Rov - er, ____ wan - d'rer,
let ring
let ring
N.C.
E5 N.C.
no - mad, vag - a- bond, call me what you will, _____________ yeah!
guitars 2 & 3
tr
Rhythm fill 1
P.M.
P.M.
tr

Pre-Chorus
A5 A#5 B5 C5 F5
N.C.
E5
Oh. _______ But I'll take my time an-y-where, _ free to
end Rhythm fill 1
Rhythm figure 4
P.M.
P.M.
P.M.
tr
tr
N.C.
Bb5
N.C.
speak my mind an-y-where. _
And I'll re-de-fine an-y-where. _
And I'll nev-er mind an-y-where. _
(cont. in slashes)
tr
tr
P.M.
P.M.
P.M.
end Rhythm figure 4
tr
tr
tr
Half time feel
Chorus
A5
G5
to Coda
6 10fr.
D
end half time feel
An-y-where I roam, _______ where I lay my head is home, _ yeah! _
with Rhythm figure 1
E5 N.C.
E5 N.C.
A5 A#5 B5 C5
N.C.
P.M.

Half time feel
D.S. al Coda
E5
F5
(Whispered:) And the earth be-comes _ my throne. _______
2. And the earth be-comes. _ my throne. _
P.M.
Coda
guitar 3
E5
Interlude
guitar 2
P.M.
tr
tr
P.M.
E5
N.C.
guitar 2
P.M.
both gtrs.
guitar 3
tr
tr
E5
N.C.
guitar 2
both gtrs.
P.M.
guitar 3
* P.M. refers to both guitars
Pre-chorus
with Rhythm figure 4
F5
N.C.
E5
N.C.
But I'll take my time an - y - where. _
I'm free to speak my mind. ________
45

Bb5
N.C.
Half time feel
Chorus
A5
And I'll take my find an-y-where. An-y-where I roam, __
G5
(end half time feel)
___________ where I lay my head is home, ___ that's where.
Guitar solo
with Rhythm figure 1 (2 times)
E5 N.C.
E5 N.C.
guitar 5
with wah
A5 A#5 B5 C5
E5
N.C.
8va
* Tap with edge of pick
8va
E5
N.C.
A5 A#5 B5 C5 D5 E5
guitars 2 & 3
Half time feel
with Rhythm figure 3
hold bend
B R P.M. B R B
46

Bb5
G5
8va
B R
T.B.
8va
Bb5
(end half time feel)
with Rhythm fill 1
N.C.
T.B.
8va
E5
N.C.
T.B.
B R B R
A5
A#5
B5
C5
D5
6 19fr.
B
8va
3
Pre-Chorus
with Rhythm figure 4
F5
N.C.
E5
But I'll take my time an-y-where. ___
I'm free to
8va
3

N.C.
Bb5
N.C.
speak my mind an - y - where. __ And I'll re - de - fine an - y - where.

Half time feel
Chorus
A5
G5
An - y- where I roam, __________ where I lay my head is home. _____

C5
B5
Bb5(type2)
(end half time feel)
6 open 3fr. 2fr.
E G F#
P.M.
Carved up - on __ my stone, _____ my bod - y ___ lie, __ but still I ___ roam, __ yeah __ yeah _

Outro
with Rhythm figure 1
E5 N.C.
with Backing vocal figure 1
E5 N.C.
A5 A#5 B5 C5
___ Wher - ev - er __ I __ may __ roam _

with Rhythm figure 2 (till fade)
N.C.
E5 N.C.
A5 A#5 B5 C5
___ Wher - ev - er ___ I ____ may roam, _

with Backing vocal figure 1
E5 N.C.
A5 A#5 B5 C5
___ roam. __________ Wher - ev - er I ___ may roam. _

Backing vocal figure 1
E5 N.C.
A5 A#5 B5 C5
Wher - ev - er ___ I ____ may roam. _____

N.C.
guitar 5
8va
with wah
* Tap with edge of pick
with vocal ad lib (till fade)
E5
N.C.
A5
A#5
B5
C5
8va
N.C.
E5
N.C.
8va
* Tap with edge of pick
A5
A#5
B5
C5
N.C.
8va
E5
N.C.

A5 A#5 B5 C5
Begin fade
N.C.
E5 N.C.
A5 A#5 B5 C5 N.C.
E5 N.C.
A5 A#5 B5 C5
N.C.
E5 N.C.
50

Additional lyrics

2. And the earth becomes my throne,
    I adapt to the unknown.
    Under wandering stars I've grown,
    By myself but not alone.
    I ask no one.
    And my ties are severed clean,
    The less I have, the more I gain.
    Off the beaten path I reign.
    Rover, wanderer, nomad, vagabond,
    Call me what you will. *(to Pre-chorus)*

DON'T TREAD ON ME

WORDS & MUSIC BY JAMES HETFIELD LARS ULRICH

end Rhythm figure 2
E5   Bb5   F5   E5   F5 G5   F5
P.M.   P.M.
guitars 1 & 2 play Rhythm figure 2 (2 times)
E5   Bb5   F5   E5   F5   E5   Bb5   F5   E5   F5   G5   F5
E5   Bb5   F5 E5   Bb5   F5   E5   Bb5   F5 E5   F5   G5   F5   E5   Bb5   F5 E5   Bb5   F5
Don't tread on me.
guitar 3
with slide
Riff A
12 11 9
0
E5   Bb5 F5 E5   F5 G5   F5   E5   Bb5   F5 E5   Bb5   F5   E5   Bb5   F5   E5 F5 G5   F5
Say, don't tread on me.
end Riff A
12 11 9 9
0
12 11 9
12 11 9 9
1st, 2nd Verse
E5   F5   F#5   G5
Rhythm figure 3
P.M.   P.M.   P.M.   P.M.   P.M.   P.M.
1. Lib - er - ty or death,   what we so proud - ly ___ hail.   Once you pro - voke her, __
2. See additional lyrics
0

end Rhythm figure 3
with Rhythm figure 2
rat - tl - ing of her __ tail. ____ Nev - er be - gins it, nev - er, but once en - gaged,
with Rhythm figure 2 (1st 2 bars only) & Fill 1
nev - er sur - ren - ders, __ show - ing the fangs of __ rage. ____
P.M.
Say, don't tread on me. ____
Chorus
with Fill 2
Rhythm figure 4
P.M.
with Fill 3
So be __ it, threat - en no more. _ To se - cure peace _ is
end Rhythm figure 4
with Rhythm figure 3 (1st 3 bars only) & Fill 2
to pre - pare for __ war. So be __ it, set - tle the score. ____
Fill 1
Fill 2
Fill 3

Touch me a-gain for the words that you will hear ev-er- more. _ Hey!
Don't tread on me.
Don't tread on me! __
Fine
Guitar solo
with Rhythm figure 2 (2 times)

E5
P.M.
8va
F5
P.M.
F#5
P.M.
G5
P.M.
G#5
P.M.
A5
Bb5
B5
D5
B
E5
P.M.
G5
E5
G5
E5
P.M.
G5
E5
P.M.
(Growled:)
Ruff.
8va
U.B.
U.B.
B
G5
E5
G5
E5
A5
E5
Bb
E
A
E
P.M.
P.M.
P.M.
P.M.
P.M.
P.M.
P.M.
E5
G5
E5
G5
E5
A5
E5
Bb
E
A
E
G
E
P.M.
P.M.
P.M.
P.M.

Additional lyrics

2. Love it or leave it, she, with the deadly bite.
   Quick is the blue tongue, forked as the lightning strike.
   Shining with brightness, always on surveillance.
   The eyes, they never close, emblem of vigilance.
   Say, don't tread on me. *(to Chorus)*

THROUGH THE NEVER

WORDS & MUSIC BY JAMES HETFIELD, LARS ULRICH & KIRK HAMMETT

58

(E5)
A5   B♭5   N.C.
U - ni-verse,   much too __ big to see. ________
slight P.M.
P.M.

(E5)
Time and space   nev - er   end- ing.   Dis-turb-ing thoughts,   ques - tions pend-ing.
P.M.

A5   B♭5   E5 N.C.(E5)
Lim - i - ta - tion of   hu-man un-der-stand-ing. ________   Too quick to __
P.M.   P.M.   P.M.

(G5)   (end half time feel) (F♯5)
crit - i - cize. _   Ob- li- ga - tion_   to   sur- vive. _   We hun - ger to
P.M.

F#5
A5
Bb5
N.C.
be a - live.
Yeah.
Riff A
end Riff A
N.C.
with Fill 1
(Twist - ing, turn - ing through the nev - er.)
P.M.
P.M.
P.M.
P.M.
P.M.
P.M.
P.M.
P.M.
P.M.
Rhythm figure 2
end Rhythm figure 2
Half time feel
Chorus
E5 F#5
E5 F#5
E5 F#5
E5 F#5
E5 F#5
All that is,
ev- er,
ev - er was
will be
ev - er
Rhythm figure 3
Fill 1
guitar 3

to Coda
(end half time feel)
E5 F#5 E5 F#5 E5 F#5 E5 F#5 G5
twist - ing, turn - ing through the nev - er.
end Rhythm figure 3
with Rhythm figure 1
N.C.
G5 N.C.
guitars 1 & 2
E5
with Riff A
N.C.
D.S. al Coda
Coda
(end half time feel)
E5 F#5 E5 F#5 N.C. E5 F5 F#5 G5 G#5
through the nev- er
guitars 1 & 2
P.M.
open 2fr. open 2fr. open 2fr. open 2fr. open 2fr. open 2fr. open 2fr. open 2fr.
A B A B A B A B A B A B A B A B C5
P.M.
guitar 1 8va
steady gliss.
B R

E5   G5   N.C.
guitar 1
with Rhythm figure 4 (both guitars)
E5   G5   N.C.
play 7 times
3
5 7 5
6
guitar 2
3
P.M.
P.M.
Rhythm figure 4
end Rhythm figure 4
2 0 0 0 3 0 0
6
5 5 7 5
6

Bridge
with Rhythm figure 4 (8 times)
E5   G5   N.C.
E5   G5   N.C.
On   through   the   nev - er.   We   must   go

E5   G5   N.C.
E5   G5   N.C.
on   through   the   nev - er,   out   to   the

E5   G5   N.C.
E5   G5   N.C.
edge   of   for - ev - er.   We   must   go

E5   G5   N.C.
E5   G5   N.C.
on   through   the   nev - er.   Then   nev - er

guitar 2
(end half time feel)
E5
comes.

guitar 1
P.M.   P.M.   P.M.   P.M.   P.M.
0 2   3   2 0 2   3   0 2   3   2 0 2   3   2

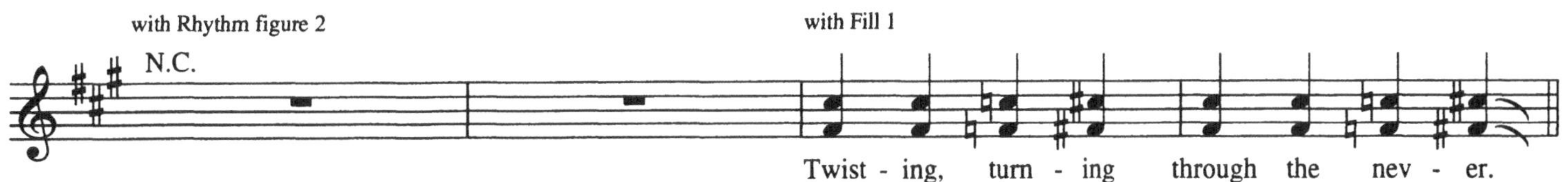

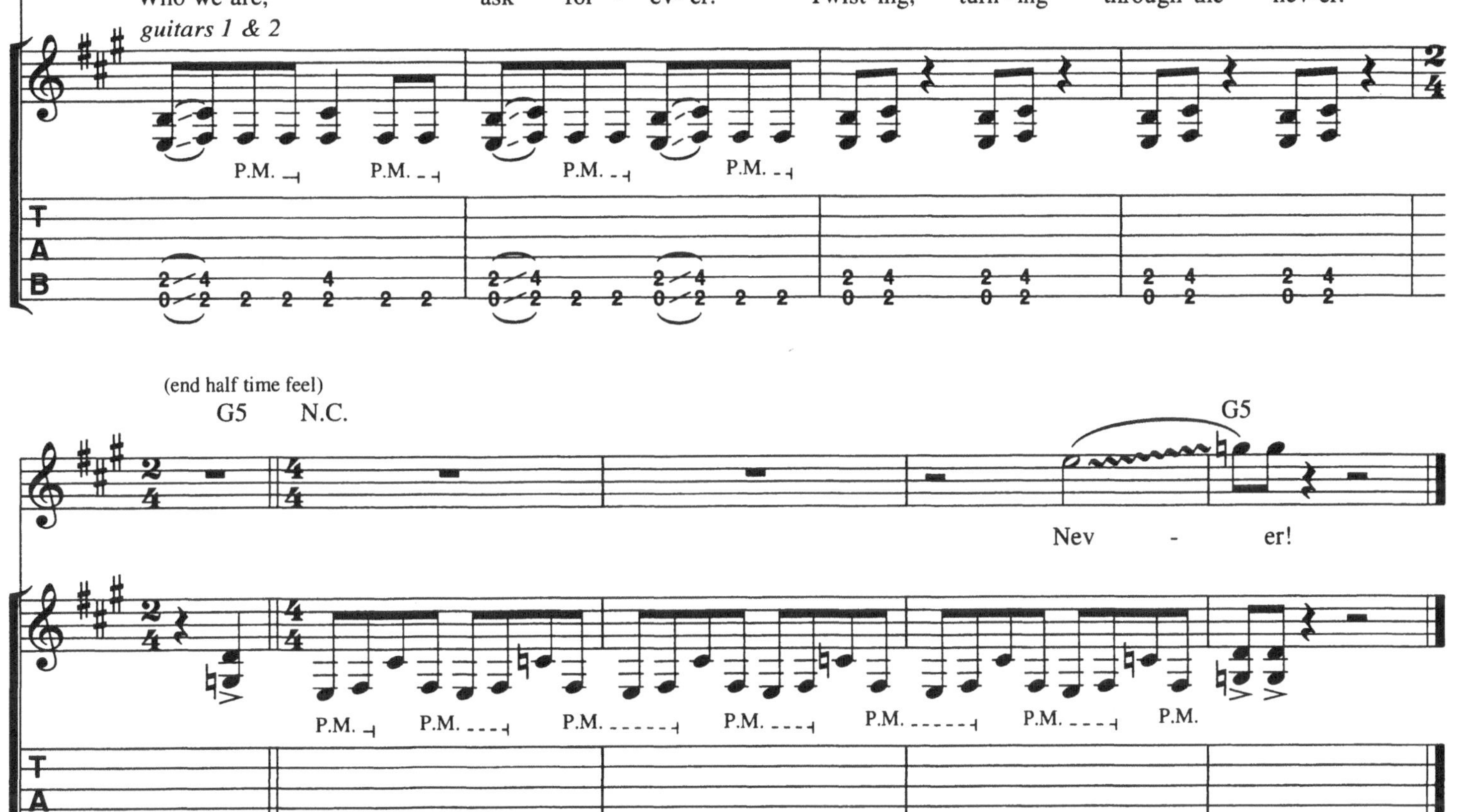

Additional lyrics

2. In the dark, see past our eyes.
Pursuit of truth, no matter where it lies.
Gazing up to the breeze of the heavens.
On a quest, meaning, reason.
Come to be, how it began.
All alone in the family of the sun.
Curiosity teasing everyone.
On our home, third stone from the sun. Yeah.

Twisting, turning through the never. *(to Chorus)*

NOTHING ELSE MATTERS

WORDS & MUSIC BY JAMES HETFIELD LARS ULRICH

Em   D   C   G   B7   Em
Rhythm figure 1
end Rhythm figure 1
guitar 2
let ring - - - - - -| simile
N.H.
T.B.
* Vol. knob swell.

1st Verse

Em   D   Dsus4   Cadd2   N.C.   Em
So close,   no mat - ter how __ far. ___________   Could - n't be much more __
guitar 1
Rhythm figure 2

D   Cadd2   N.C.   Em   D
from   the heart. _____   For - ev -er trust - ing who we are. ___________

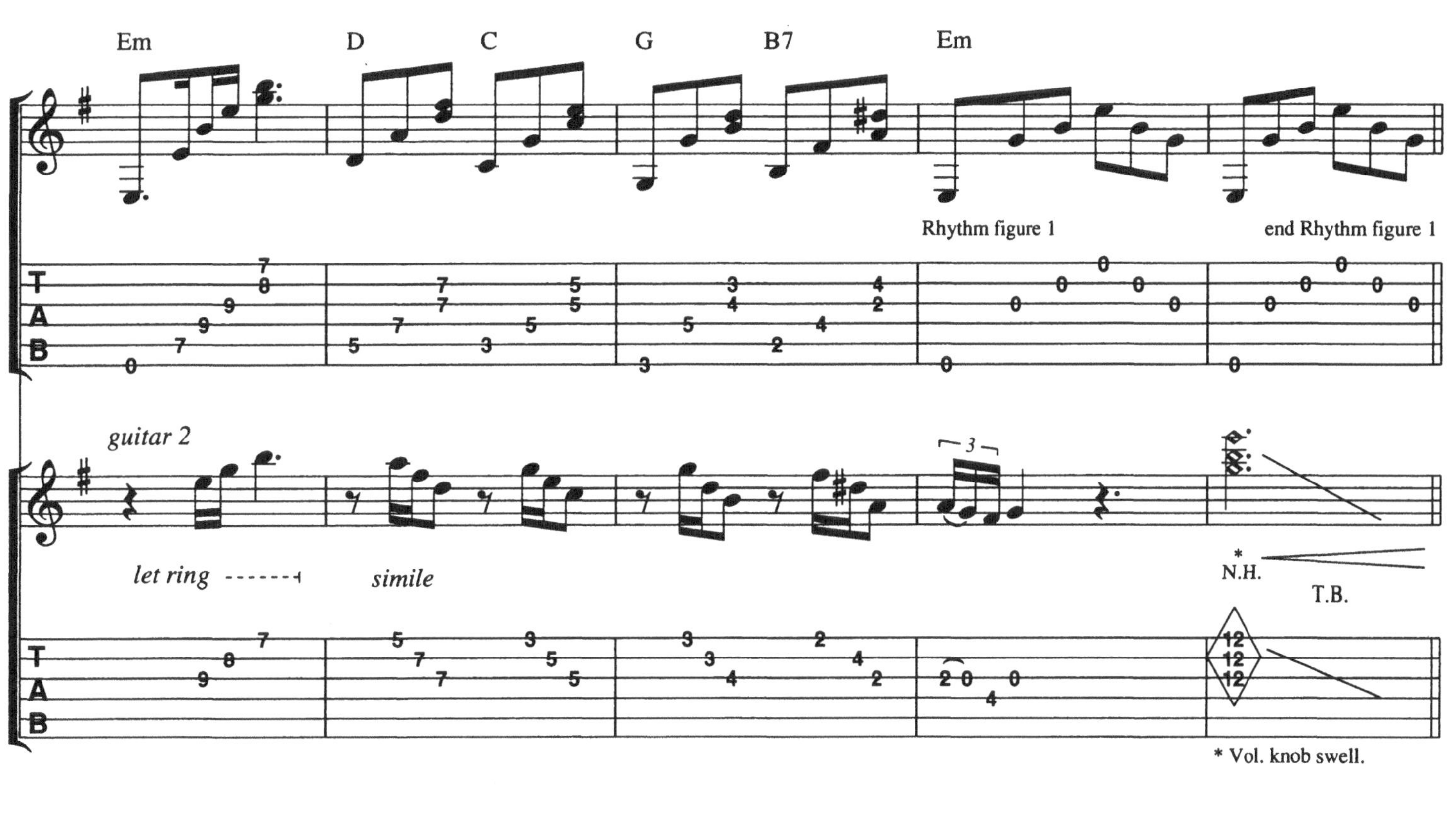

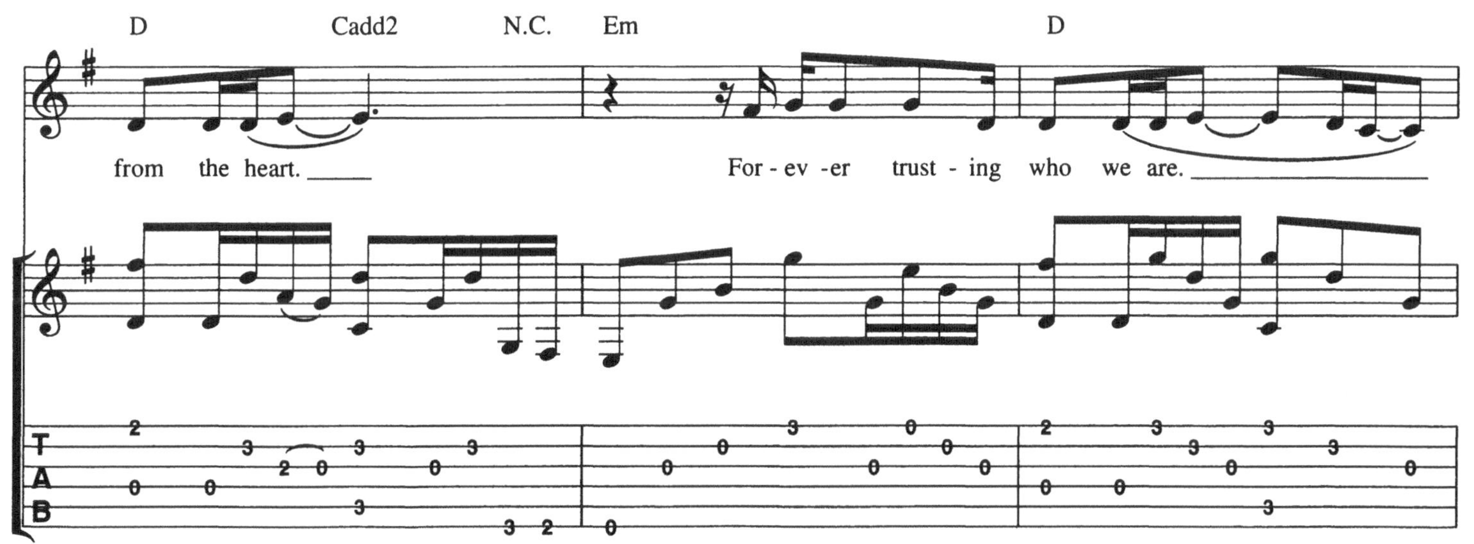

2nd Verse
with Rhythm figure 2
G   B7   Em   N.C.   Em
And noth-ing else _ mat-ters. _______
Rhy. fig. 2A
guitar 3 (with distortion)
guitar 4 (with distortion)
end Rhythm figure 2
Rhythm figure 3
Nev - er o - pened my -
D Dsus4 Cadd2   N.C. Em   D   Cadd2 N.C. Em
self this way. _____
Life is ours, we live it our way. _______
All _ these words I don't
D   Dsus4   Cadd2   G   B7   Em
with Rhythm figure 2A
just say. _________
And noth-ing else _ mat-ters. _______
end Rhythm figure 3
3rd Verse
with Rhythm figure 2
Em   D Dsus4 Cadd2 N.C. Em   D   Cadd2
Trust I seek and I find in __ you. __
Ev - 'ry day _ for us __ some - thing new. _____
guitar 2 (clean)
Rhythm figure 4

Em
D   Dsus4 Cadd2   G   B7
O - pen mind _ for a dif - f'rent view. ____   And noth - ing else __
end Rhythm figure 4
Em
guitars 1 & 6*
Chorus
C   A   D   Dsus4 D Dadd2   D
* guitar 2
mat - ters. ___________   Nev - er cared for what __ they
* Synthesizer arranged for guitar
* guitar 6 is acoustic
with Rhythm fill 1
C   A   D   Dsus4 D Dadd2   D   C   A
Rhythm figure 5
do. ____________   Nev - er cared for what _ they know, __________
with Rhy. fig. 1 & Rhy. fill 1
D   Em
guitar 6
4th Verse
end Rhythm figure 5
with Rhythm figure 2
oh,   but   I   know. ___________   So close, no mat - ter
Rhythm fill 1   Em
(guitar 5 *)
* Synthesizer arranged for guitar
69

D Dsus4 Cadd2 N.C. Em   D   Cadd2 N.C.
how __ far. ______   Could - n't be much more __ from   the heart. ______

Em   D   Dsus4 Cadd2 G   B7   Em
___ For - ev - er trust - ing who we are. ______ And noth - ing else _ mat - ters. ______

guitars   C   A   with Rhythm figure 5
1 & 4   D   Dsus4 D Dadd2   D   C   A   D   Dsus4 D Dadd2   D
                     Nev - er cared for what _ they do. ______   Nev - er cared for what _ they

with Rhythm fill 2
C   A   D   Em   with Rhythm figure 1 & Rhythm fill 3
know, ____________   oh,   but   I   know. ______

N.C. (Em)   Am
8va
guitar 2

guitar 1 let ring
* guitar 2 notated to left of slashes

Rhythm fill 2
C   A   D   Em
guitar 3
with distortion

Rhythm fill 3
Em
guitar 5*

* Synthesis arranged for guitar

1.
C   Dadd2   Em

2. with Fill 1
Dadd2   Em
guitar 1

5th Verse
with Rhythm figures 2 & 3
D   Dsus4   Cadd2   N.C.   Em
I nev-er o-pened my-self this way. _____ Life is ours, we live it

D   Cadd2   3   N.C.   Em   D   Dadd2   Cadd2
our way. _______ All ___these words I don't just say. _________

G   B7   Em   w/Rhy. Fig. 2A
And noth-ing else __ mat-ters. _______________

6th Verse
with Rhythm figures 2 & 4
Em   D   Dsus4   Cadd2 N.C. Em
Trust I seek and I find in __ you. _____ Ev-'ry day __ for __ us

Fill 1   guitar 2 (clean)
Dadd2   Em
6/8
B R   B   B R
3

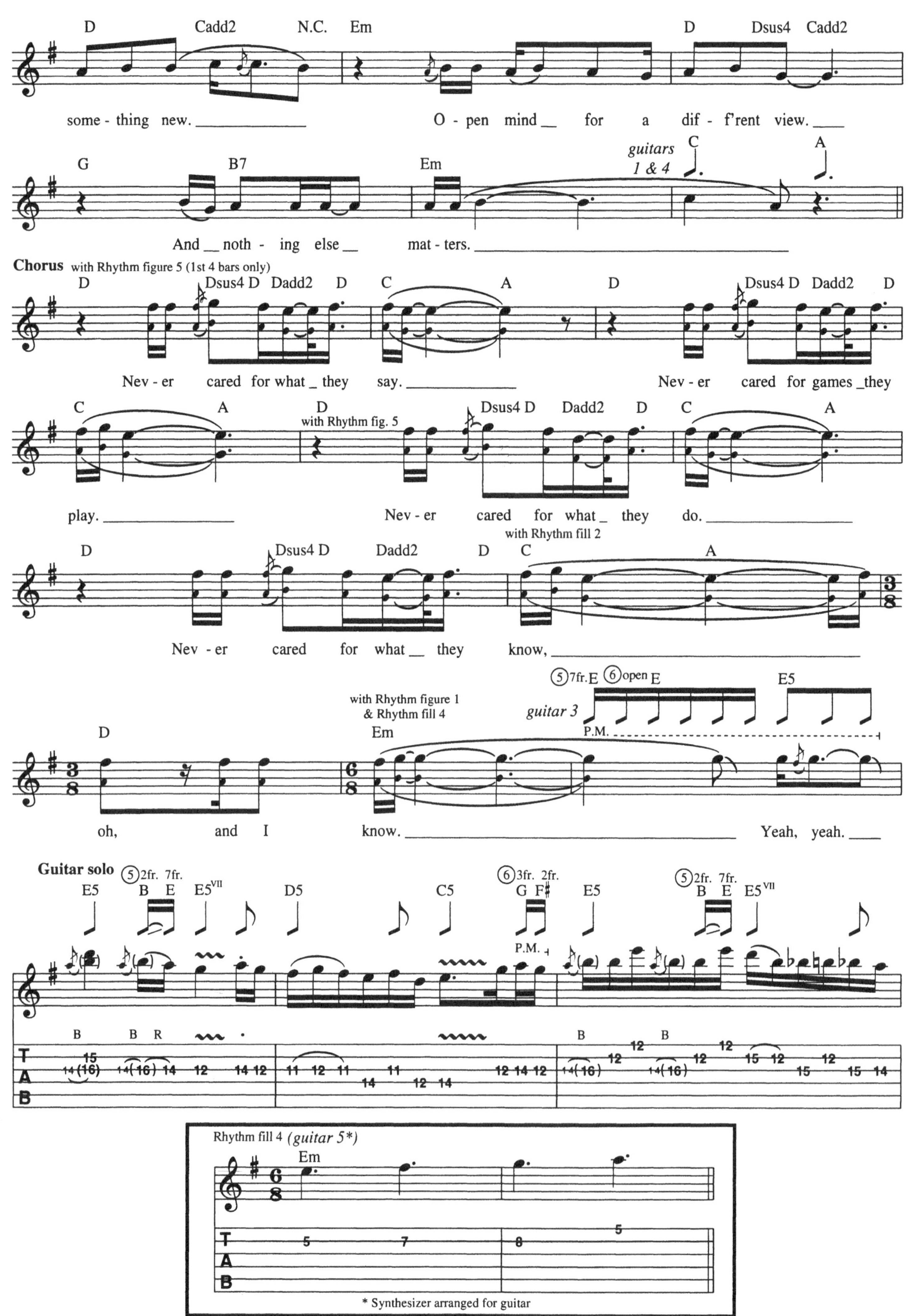

D   Cadd2   N.C.   Em   D   Dsus4   Cadd2
some - thing new. _______   O - pen mind __ for a dif - f'rent view. ___
G   B7   Em   guitars 1 & 4   C   A
And __ noth - ing else __ mat - ters. _______________________
Chorus with Rhythm figure 5 (1st 4 bars only)
D   Dsus4 D Dadd2 D   C   A   D   Dsus4 D Dadd2 D
Nev - er cared for what _ they say. _______   Nev - er cared for games _ they
C   A   D   with Rhythm fig. 5   Dsus4 D Dadd2 D   C   A
play. _______   Nev - er cared for what _ they do. _______
with Rhythm fill 2
D   Dsus4 D   Dadd2 D   C   A   3/8
Nev - er cared for what _ they know, _______________
(5) 7fr. E (6) open E   E5
guitar 3   P.M.
with Rhythm figure 1 & Rhythm fill 4
D   Em
3/8   6/8
oh,   and I   know. _______________   Yeah, yeah. ___
Guitar solo
(5) 2fr. 7fr.
E5   B E E5 VII   D5   C5   (6) 3fr. 2fr. G F#   E5   (5) 2fr. 7fr. B E E5 VII
P.M.
B   B R   B   B
T
15   14(16) 14(16) 14   12   14 12   11 12 11   11   12 14 12   14(16)   14(16)   12 12   12   15 12   12
A
14   12 14   15   15 14
B
Rhythm fill 4 (guitar 5*)
Em
6/8
T   5   7   8   5
A
B
* Synthesizer arranged for guitar

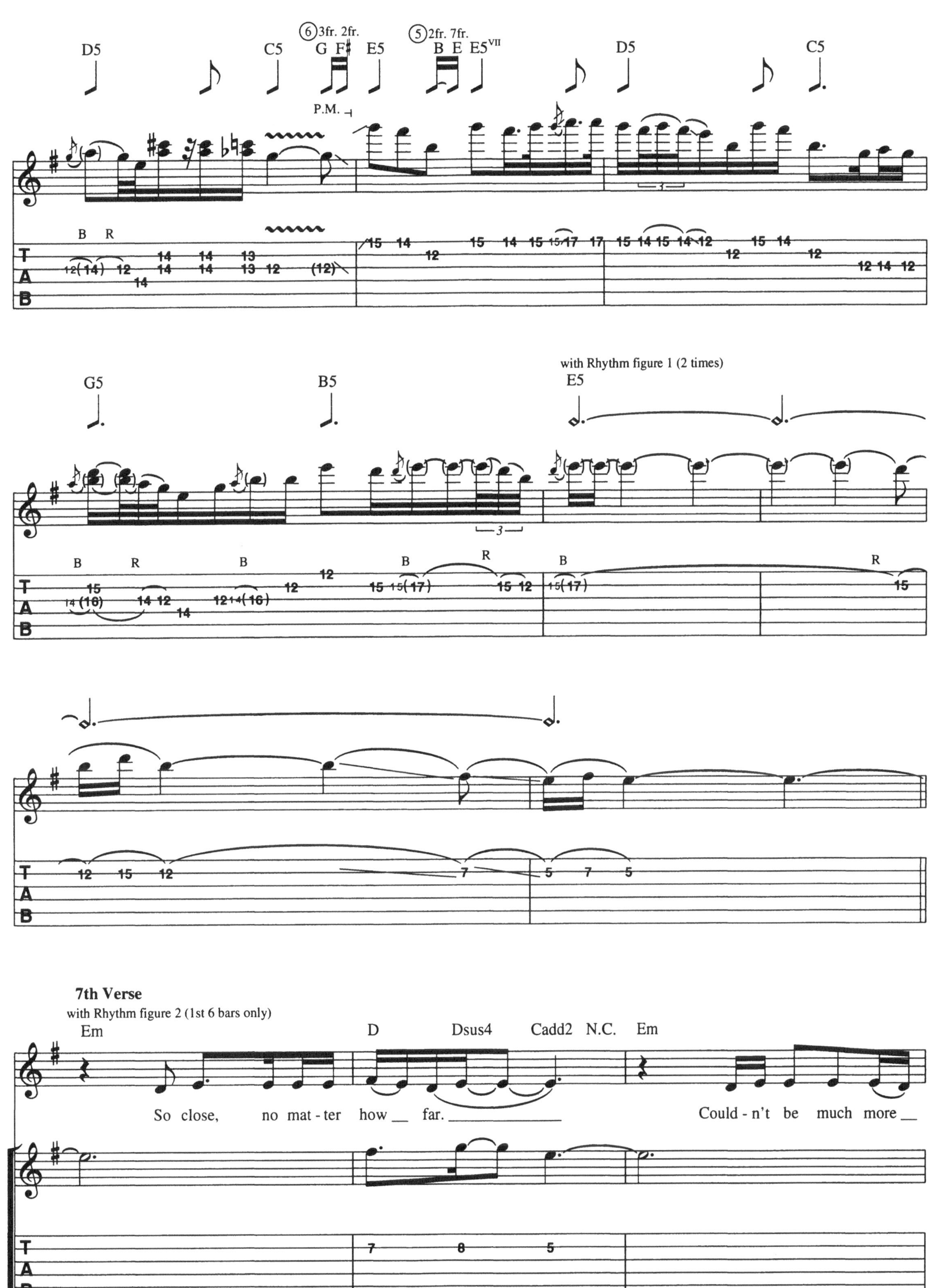

D5   C5   G F# E5   B E E5 VII   D5   C5
⑥3fr. 2fr.   ⑤2fr. 7fr.
P.M.
G5   B5   E5
with Rhythm figure 1 (2 times)
7th Verse
with Rhythm figure 2 (1st 6 bars only)
Em   D   Dsus4   Cadd2 N.C.   Em
So close,   no mat-ter how __ far. __________   Could-n't be much more __

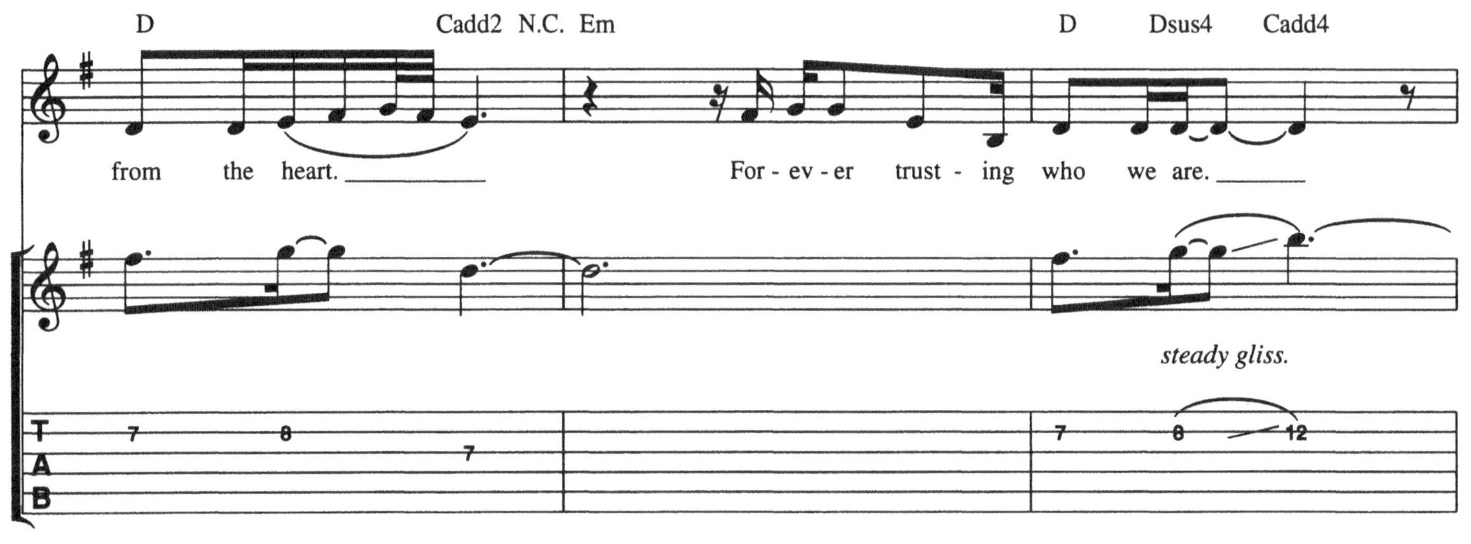

D
Cadd2 N.C. Em
D Dsus4 Cadd4
from the heart.
For - ev - er trust - ing who we are.
steady gliss.
G
B7
Em
No, noth - ing else mat - ters.
let ring till end
guitar 1

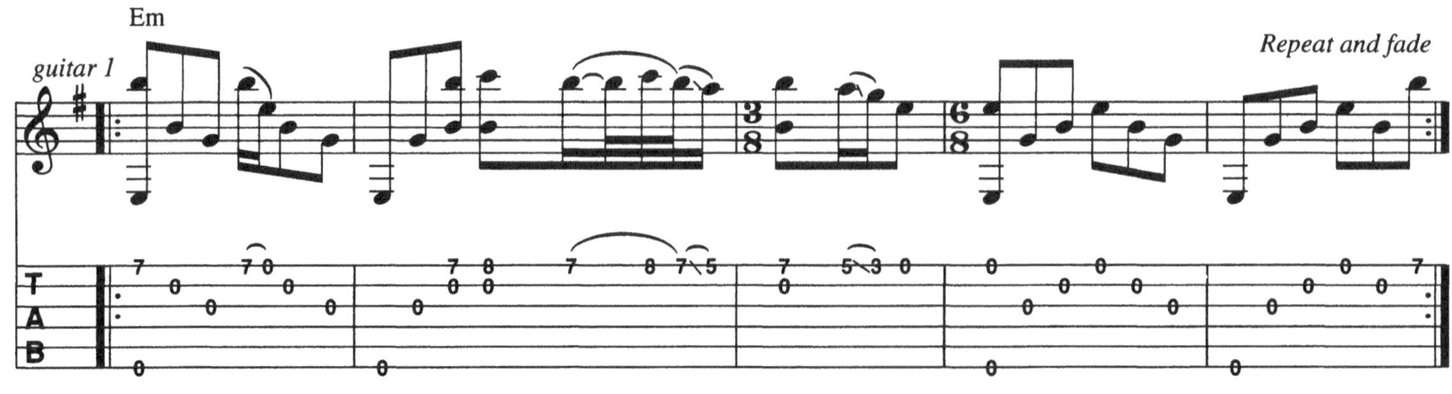

Em
guitar 1
Repeat and fade

OF WOLF AND MAN

WORDS & MUSIC BY JAMES HETFIELD, LARS ULRICH & KIRK HAMMETT

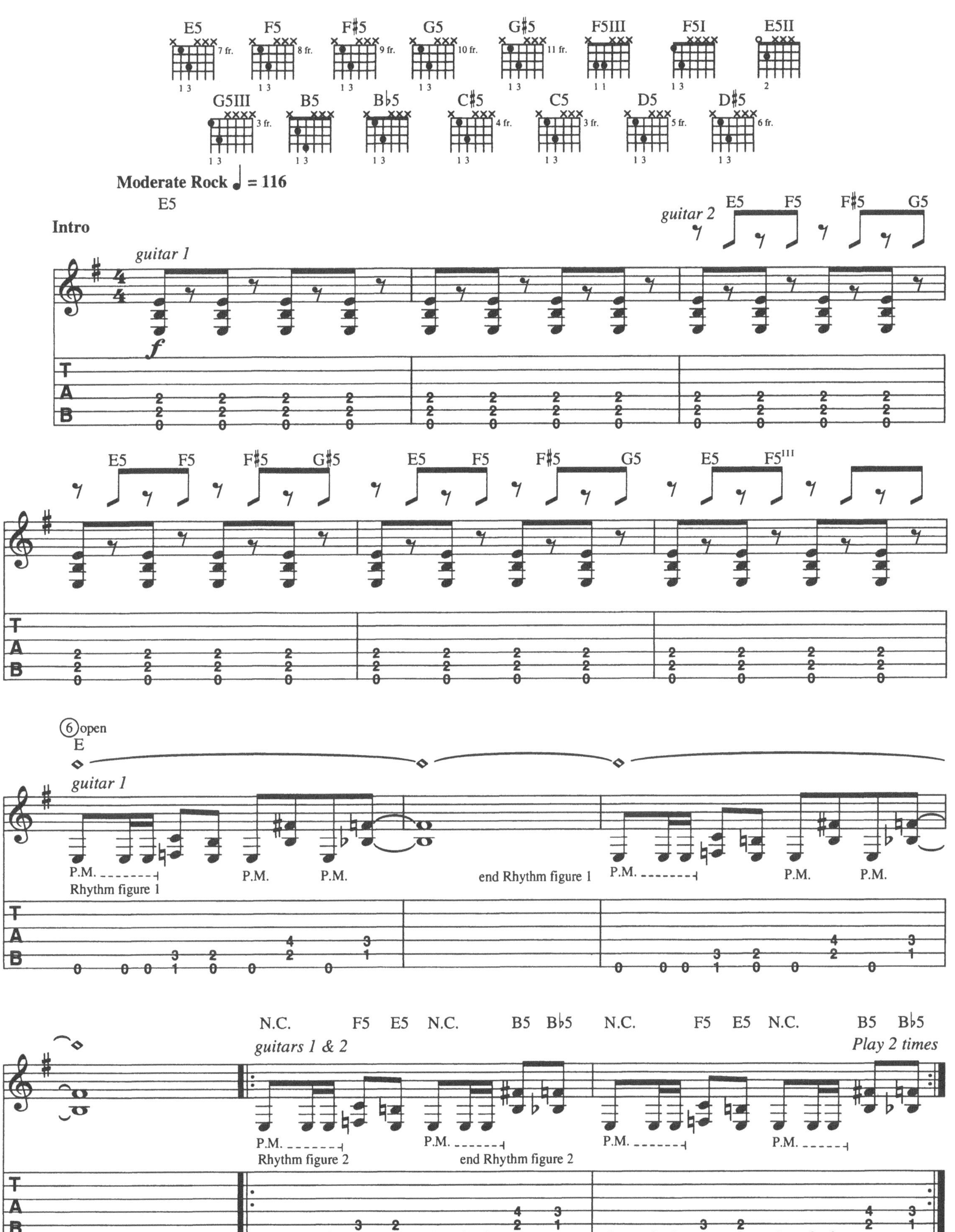

1st Verse
with Rhythm figure 2 (8 times)
N.C.   F5 E5 N.C.   B5 Bb5 N.C.   F5 E5 N.C.   B5 Bb5 N.C.   F5 E5 N.C.   B5 Bb5
Off through the new day's __ mist I ____ run. __ Out from the new day's __ mist I __

N.C.   F5 E5 N.C.   B5 Bb5 N.C.   F5 E5 N.C. B5 Bb5 N.C.   F5 E5 N.C. B5 Bb5
__ have come. ________ I hunt, ____ there -fore I am. ____

N.C.   F5   E5   N.C.   B5 Bb5 N.C.   F5 E5 N.C.   B5   Bb5
Har - vest the land. ____ Tak - ing of the fal len ___ lamb. __

N.C.   F5 E5   B5 Bb5   N.C.   F5 E5   B5 Bb5 N.C.

guitar 1 & 2
P.M. - - - -   P.M.   P.M.   P.M. - -
Rhythm figure 3   end Rhythm figure 3

2nd, 3rd Verses
with Rhythm figure 3 (4 times)
N.C.   F5 E5   B5 Bb5   N.C.   F5 E5   B5 Bb5
2. Off through the new day's __ mist I ____ run. __ Out from the new day's __ mist I __
3. See additional lyrics

N.C.   F5 E5   B5 Bb5   N.C.
__ have come. ___ We shift, ___ puls - ing with the earth. __

F5 E5   B5 Bb5   N.C.
Com - pa - ny we keep. roam - ing the land while ____ you __________

guitar 2
E5 F5 F#5 G5   B5   Bb5   Chorus   E5   F5 E5   B5   Bb5
___ sleep.   Oh. ___________   Shape shift. __   Nose to the wind. __
guitar 1
P.M.   P.M.   P.M.   P.M.

E5   F5 E5   C#5   C5   F#5   G5 F#5   C#5   C5
Shape shift. __   Feel- ing I've been. __   Move swift. __   All sens-es clean. ___________
P.M.   P.M.   P.M.   P.M.

to Coda   N.C.(F#5)   G5 F#5 N.C.(F#5)   G5 F#5
___ Earth's gift. __   (Back to the mean-ing.) back to the mean-ing   of ___   life.
P.M. - - - - - - -| P.M. - - - - - - -|

1.
with Rhythm figure 3 (2 times)
N.C. F5 E5   B5 Bb5   N.C.   F5 E5   B5 Bb5   N.C.
2.
with Rhythm figure 2 (4 times)
N.C. F5 E5 N.C. B5 Bb5

with Rhythm figure 2
⑥ open
N.C. F5 E5 N.C. B5 B♭5 N.C. F5 E5 N.C. B5 B♭5 N.C. F5 E5 N.C. B5 B♭5 E
guitar 2
⑥ open
Rhythm E   F5 I F5 II   ⑥ open E   F5 I F5 II   ⑥ open E
figure 4
guitar 1
P.M.   P.M.   P.M.   P.M.
guitar 2
3   6   (15ma) 6 (15ma) 6   6
A.H.   A.H.
F5 I F5 II   ⑥ open E   G5 III   F5 I end Rhythm figure 4
P.M.   P.M.
B
⑥ open E   F5 I F5 II   ⑥ open E   F5 I F5 II   ⑥ open E
B
3   6   6   6   6
F5 I F5 II ⑥ open E   G5 III   F5 I
B   B   B   B   B   B

E5 II   E5 I E5 II   6 open E B5   6 open E Bb5
P.M.   P.M.
C#5   C5
C5   C#5   D5   D#5   N.C.   F5 E5   B5   Bb5
w/Rhythm figure 3 (1 1/2 times)
hold bend ---
B   B   B   B
N.C.   F5   E5   B5   Bb5
R
N.C.   G5   F#5
with echo repeats
P.M.

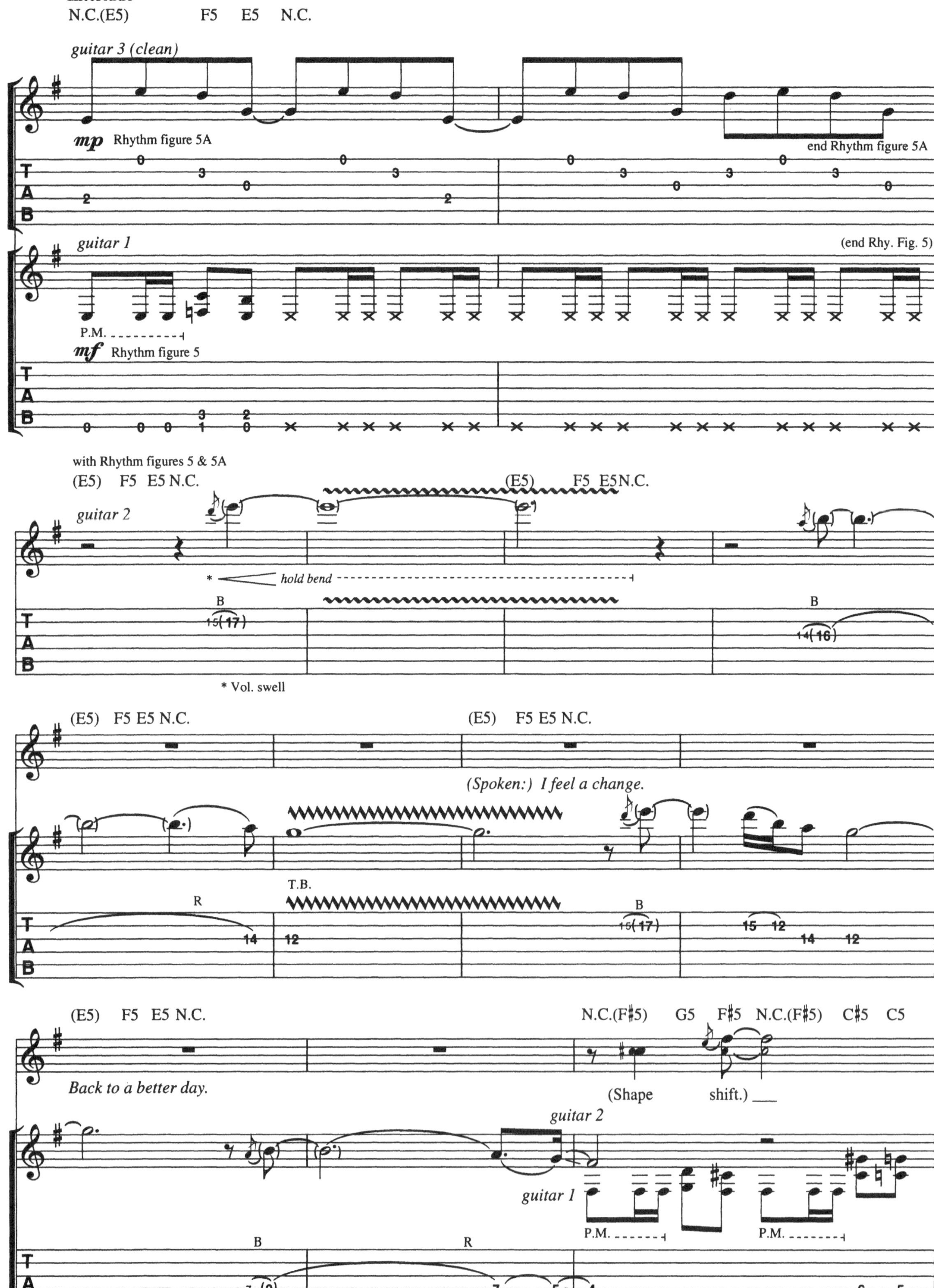

Interlude
N.C.(E5)   F5   E5   N.C.
guitar 3 (clean)
mp   Rhythm figure 5A
end Rhythm figure 5A
guitar 1
(end Rhy. Fig. 5)
P.M.
mf   Rhythm figure 5
with Rhythm figures 5 & 5A
(E5)   F5   E5 N.C.
(E5)   F5   E5 N.C.
guitar 2
*   hold bend
* Vol. swell
(E5)   F5   E5 N.C.
(E5)   F5   E5 N.C.
(Spoken:) I feel a change.
T.B.
(E5)   F5   E5 N.C.
N.C.(F#5)   G5   F#5   N.C.(F#5)   C#5   C5
Back to a better day.
(Shape   shift.)
guitar 2
guitar 1
P.M.
P.M.
80

N.C.(F#5) G5 F#5 N.C.(F#5) C#5 C5 N.C.(F#5) G5 F#5 N.C.(F#5) C#5 C5 N.C.(F#5) G5 F#5 N.C.(F#5) C#5 C5
The hair stands on the back of my neck.
(Shape shift.)
In wildness is the preservation of the world,
(cont. in slashes)
P.M.
D.S. al Coda
guitar 1
B5 C5 C#5 D5 C5 C#5 D5 D#5
(6) open E B5 (6) open E Bb5
guitar 2
8va
so seek the wolf in thyself.
T.B.* N.H.
with echo repeats
* Depress bar before striking notes at 12th fret, then return gradually to normal positon
Coda
N.C.(F#5) G5 F#5 N.C.(F#5) G5 F#5 B5 Bb5
(Back to the mean - ing,) back to the mean - ing
of wolf
P.M.
C#5 C5 C5 C#5 D5 D#5
and man,
yeah.

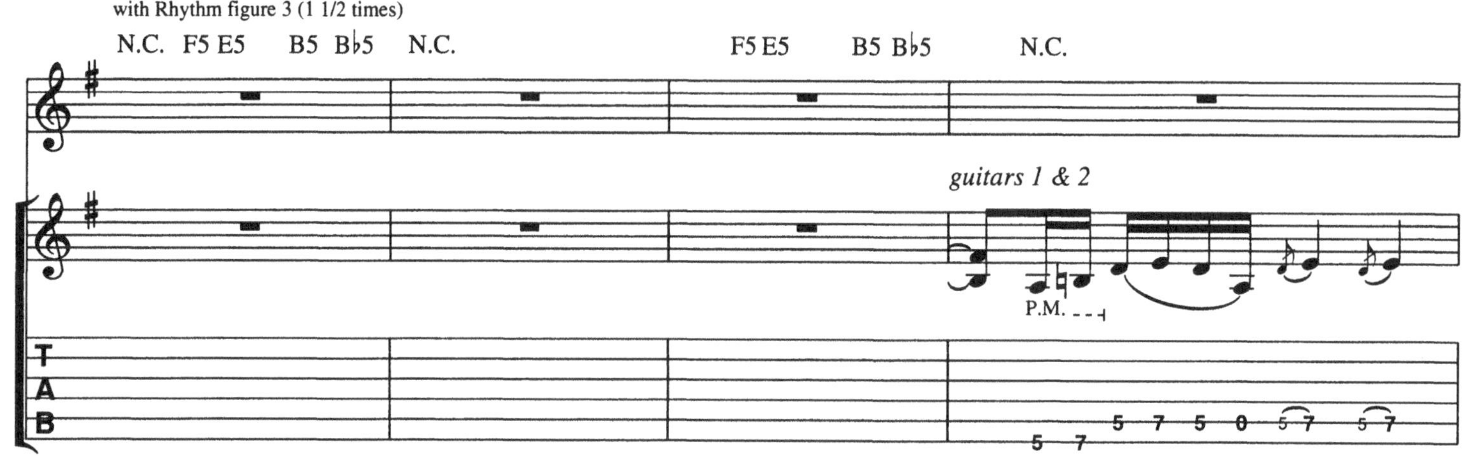

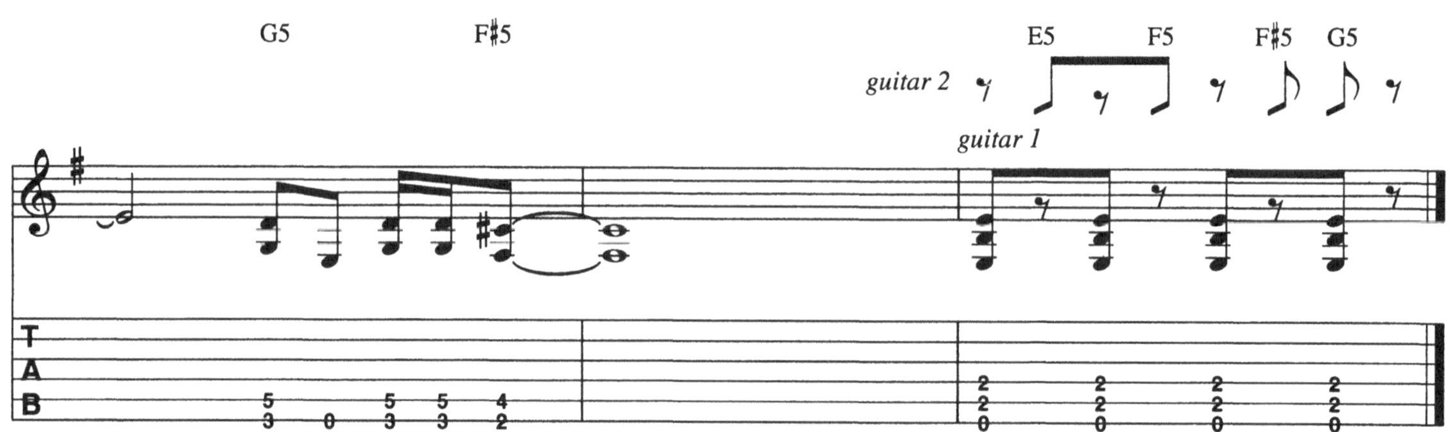

Additional lyrics

3. Bright is the moon, high in starlight.

   Chill in the air, cold as steel tonight.

   We shift. Call of the wild.

   Fear in your eyes. It's later than you realized.   *(to Chorus)*

THE GOD THAT FAILED

WORDS & MUSIC BY JAMES HETFIELD LARS ULRICH

1st, 2nd Verses
2nd time substitute Rhy. fill 1
F5 E5   F5   E5   F5 E5   G5   E5   F5 E5   F5 E5   F5   E5

1. Pride you took, _ pride you feel, _   pride that you _ felt when you'd kneel. _   Not the word, _   not the love, _
2. Find your peace, find your say, _   find the smooth _ road on _ your way. _   Trust you gave _   a child to save,

P.M.   P.M.   P.M.   P.M.   P.M.   P.M.
Rhythm figure 1   end Rhythm figure 1

F5 E5   G5   E5   E5 F5   F5   G5   N.C. F5

not what you_ thought from _ a - bove. _   It feeds,   it grows,   it clouds all that you will know. _
left you cold _ and him _ in grave. _   (It feeds.)   (It grows.)

P.M.   P.M.   P.M.   P.M.   P.M.   P.M.   P.M.

G5   E5   N.C.(Em)

De - ceit,   de - ceive,   de - cide just what you _ be - lieve. _

P.M.   P.M.   P.M.   P.M.   P.M.

Chorus
N.C.(Em)   E5   G5

I   see   faith   in your eyes. ____

N.C.(Bm)
B5
A5
N.C.(Em)
Nev- er you hear the dis-cour-ag-ing lies. _______ I hear faith in your cries. _
Rhythm figure 2
E5 G5
N.C.(Bm)
(B)
to Coda
Bro-ken is the prom-ise. Be-tray-al. _ The heal- ing hand _ held back by the deep-ened nail. _
end Rhythm figure 2
1.
with Riff A
N.C.(Em)
Fol- low the god that failed. ________
2.
G5
guitars 1 & 2
E5
B5
Fol- low the god ___ that failed. ________________ Yeah.
(guitars 1 & 2 cont. in slashes)
guitar 3
tr
tr
tr

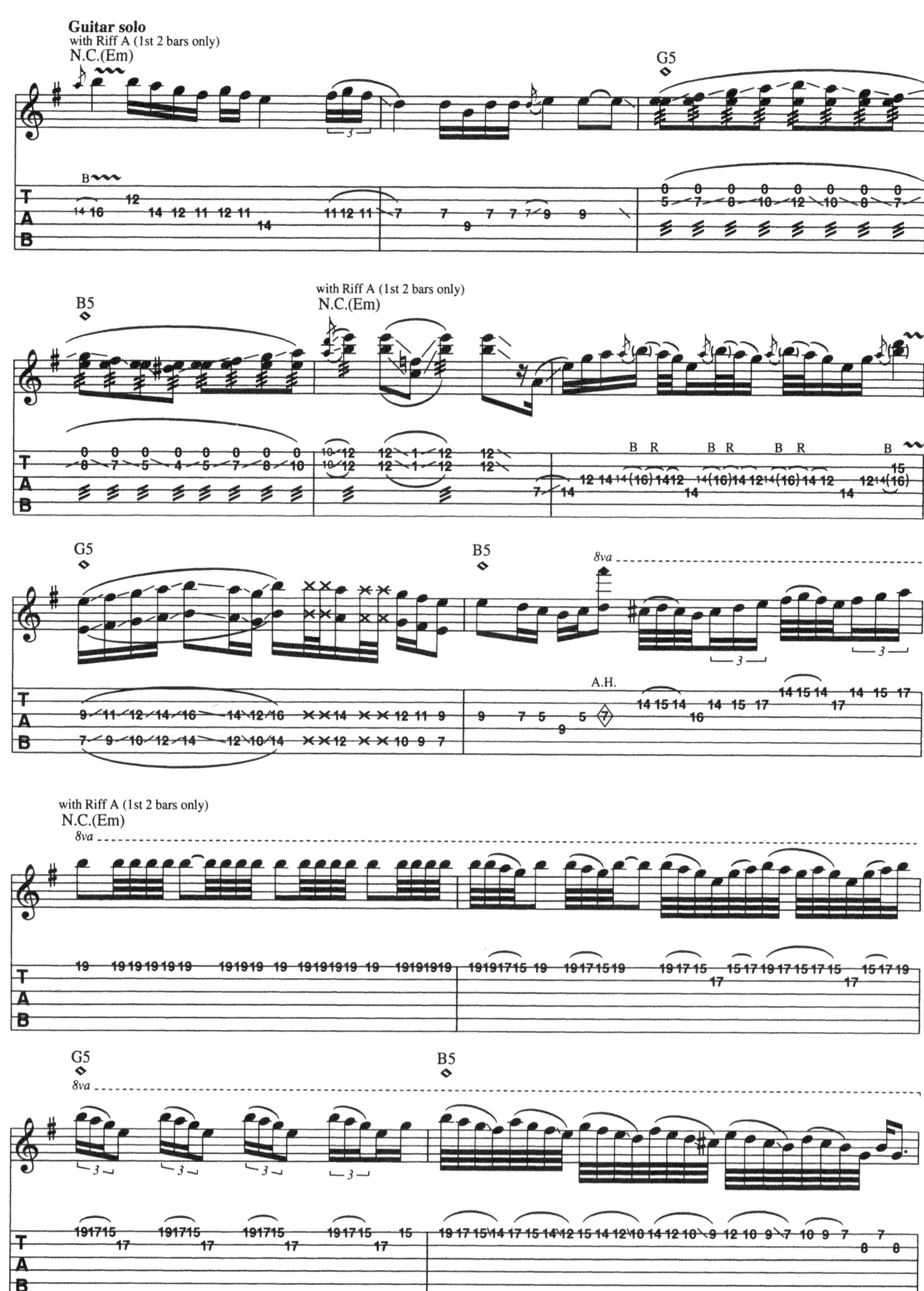

Guitar solo
with Riff A (1st 2 bars only)
N.C.(Em)
G5
B5
with Riff A (1st 2 bars only)
N.C.(Em)
G5
B5
8va
A.H.
with Riff A (1st 2 bars only)
N.C.(Em)
8va
G5
B5
8va

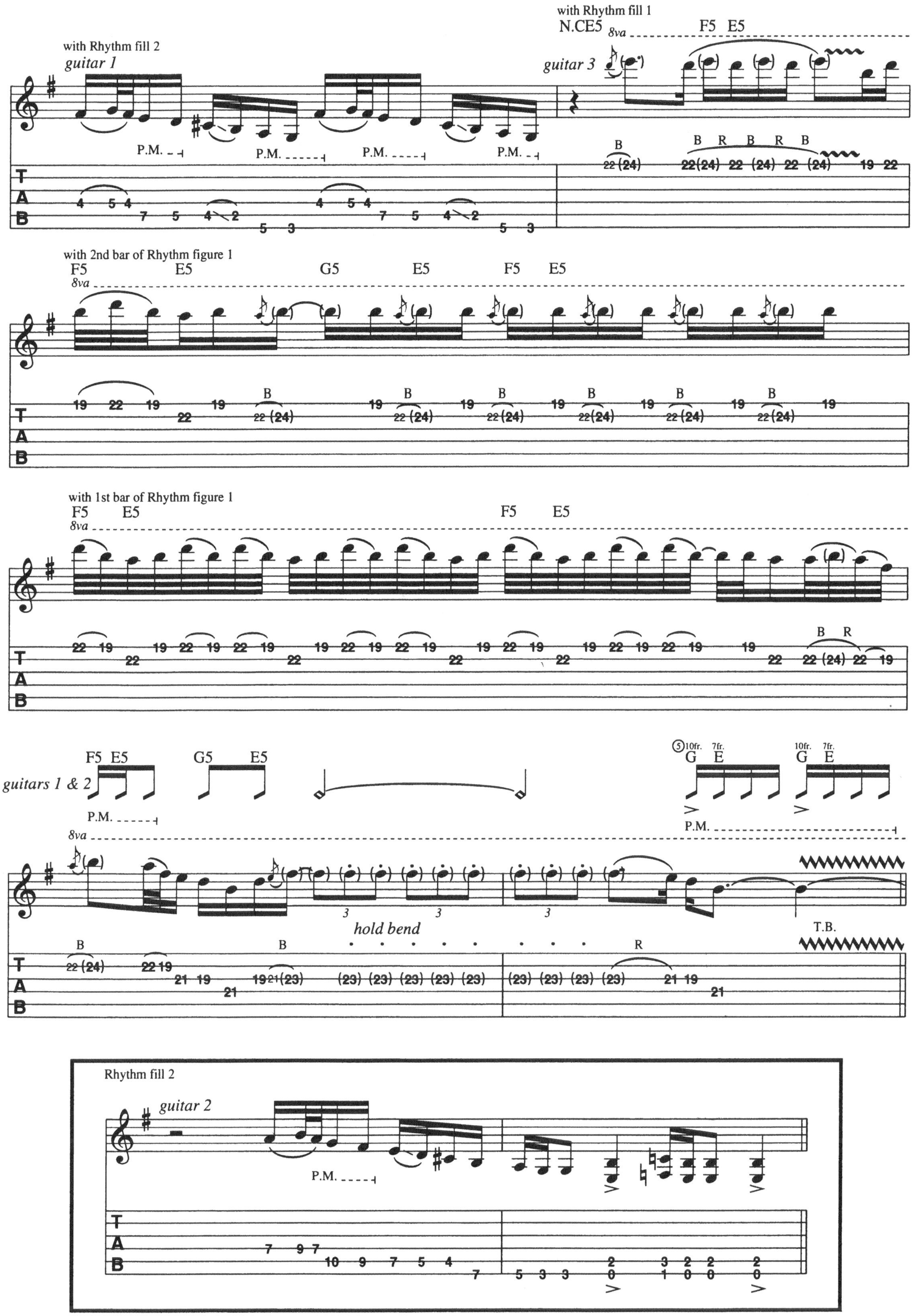
with Rhythm fill 2
guitar 1
P.M.
with Rhythm fill 1
N.CE5
8va
F5 E5
guitar 3
B R B R B
with 2nd bar of Rhythm figure 1
F5 E5 G5 E5 F5 E5
with 1st bar of Rhythm figure 1
F5 E5 F5 E5
guitars 1 & 2
F5 E5 G5 E5
G E G E
10fr. 7fr.
hold bend
T.B.
Rhythm fill 2
guitar 2

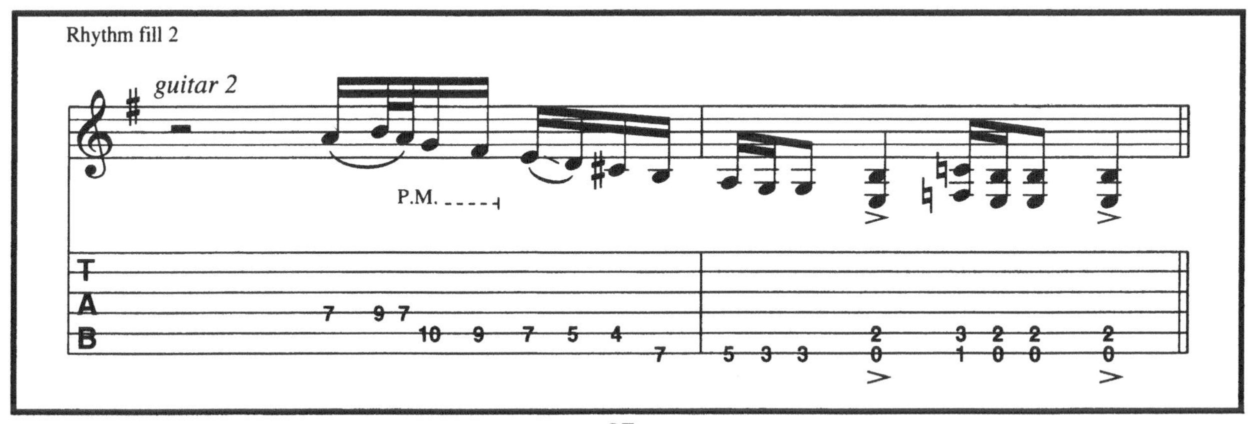

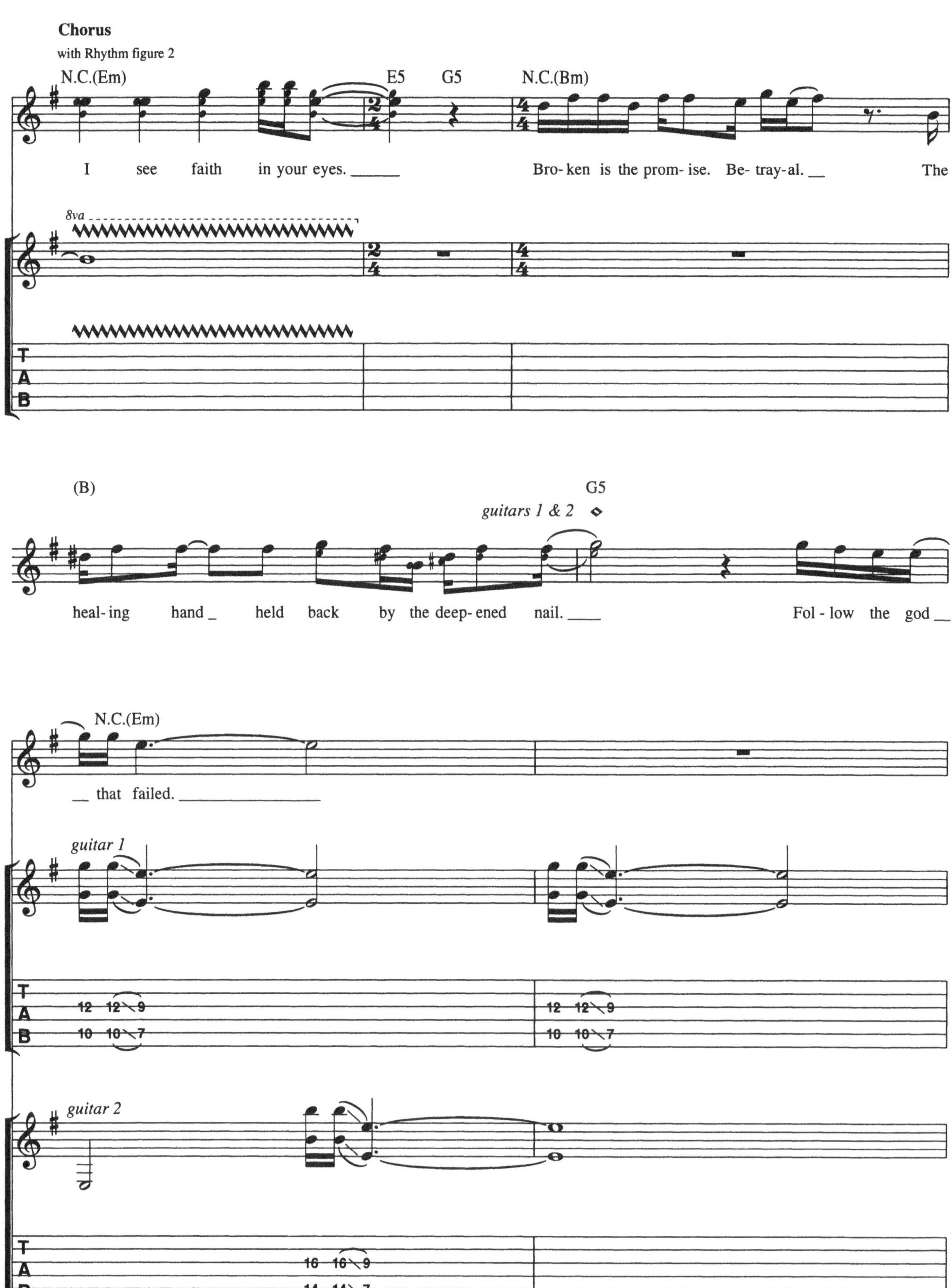

Chorus
with Rhythm figure 2
N.C.(Em)
E5
G5
N.C.(Bm)
I see faith in your eyes. Bro-ken is the prom-ise. Be-tray-al. __ The
8va
(B)
G5
guitars 1 & 2
heal-ing hand _ held back by the deep-ened nail. ___ Fol-low the god _
N.C.(Em)
__ that failed. ______
guitar 1
12 12 9
10 10 7
12 12 9
10 10 7
guitar 2
16 16 9
14 14 7
0

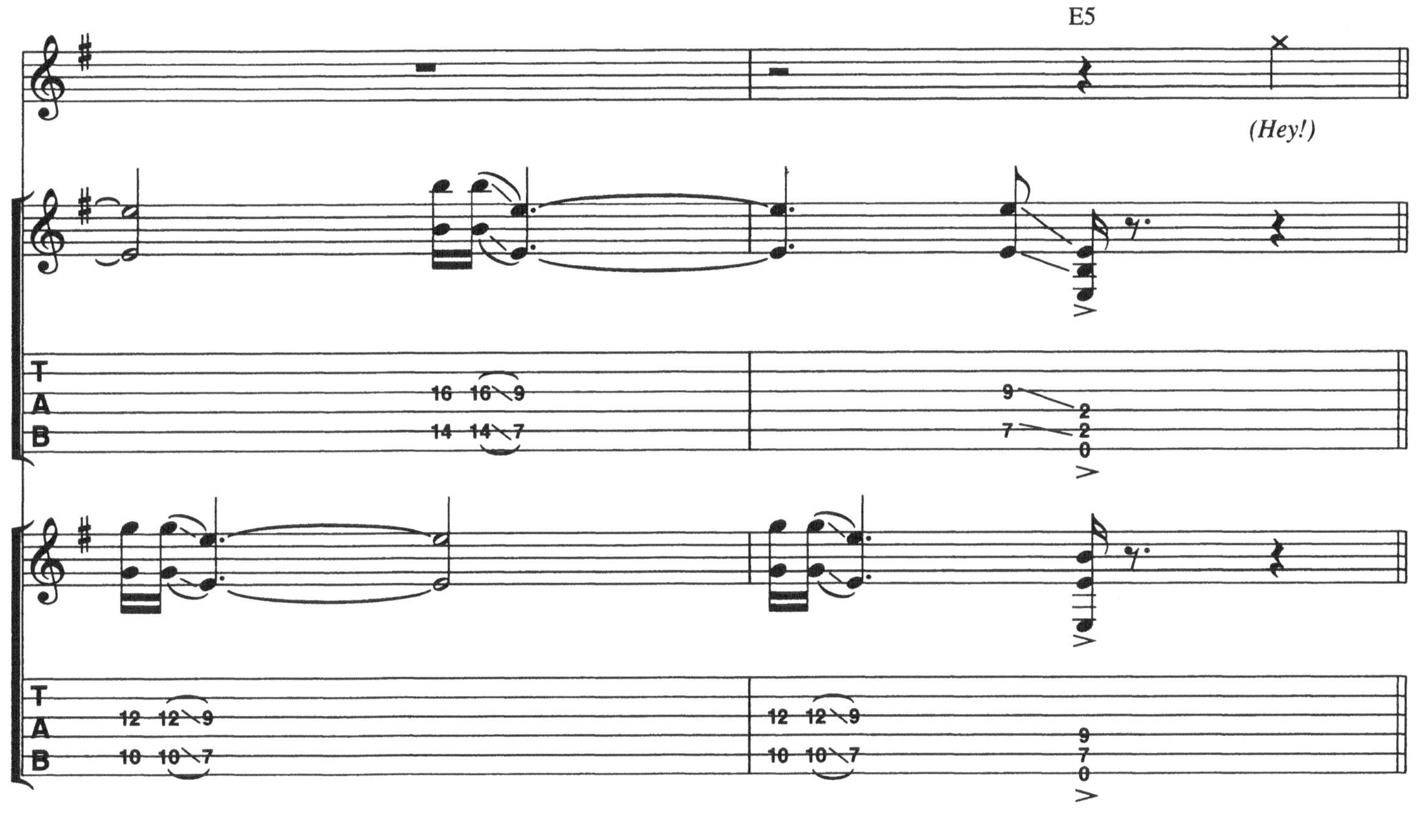

3rd Verse

with Rhythm figure 1 (2 times)

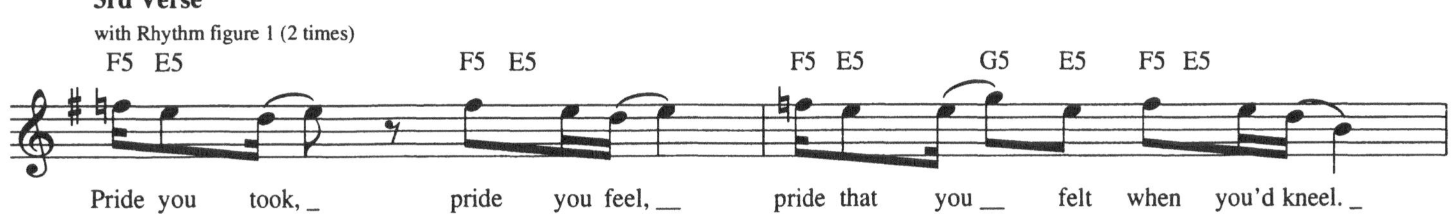

Coda

(Bm)
Fol- low the god ___ that failed. ___
P.M.
P.M.
(Em)
Bro-ken is the prom-ise. _
Be- tray-al, _
be- tray-al, _
P.M.
N.C.
with Fill 1
Em
yeah.
guitar 1
P.M.
P.M.
P.M.
P.M.
P.M.
rit.
molto rit.
guitar 5 (clean)
mp
freely
let ring
P.M.
guitar 2
P.M.
P.M.
rit.
molto rit.
Fill 1
guitar 4
Em
guitar 3
P.M.

MY FRIEND OF MISERY

WORDS & MUSIC BY JAMES HETFIELD, LARS ULRICH & JASON NEWSTED

with Rhythm figure 1 (1st 3 bars only)
Dm/A
Am
with Rhythm fill 1
P.M.
P.M.
P.M.
P.M.
end Rhythm figure 2
1st, 2nd Verses
2nd time with Riff A (3 times)
Dm/A
Am
1. You just stood there scream - ing, _______ fear - ing
2. See additional lyrics
guitars 1 & 2
Rhythm figure 3 P.M.
P.M.
P.M.
Dm/A
no one was lis - ten - ing to you. They say the emp - ty can rat - tles the most. _
P.M.
end Rhythm figure 3
P.M.
Rhythm figure 4
P.M.
Rhythm fill 1
guitar 2
Dm/A
P.M.
Riff A
guitar 3
Dm/A
Dm/A
mp
let ring
let ring

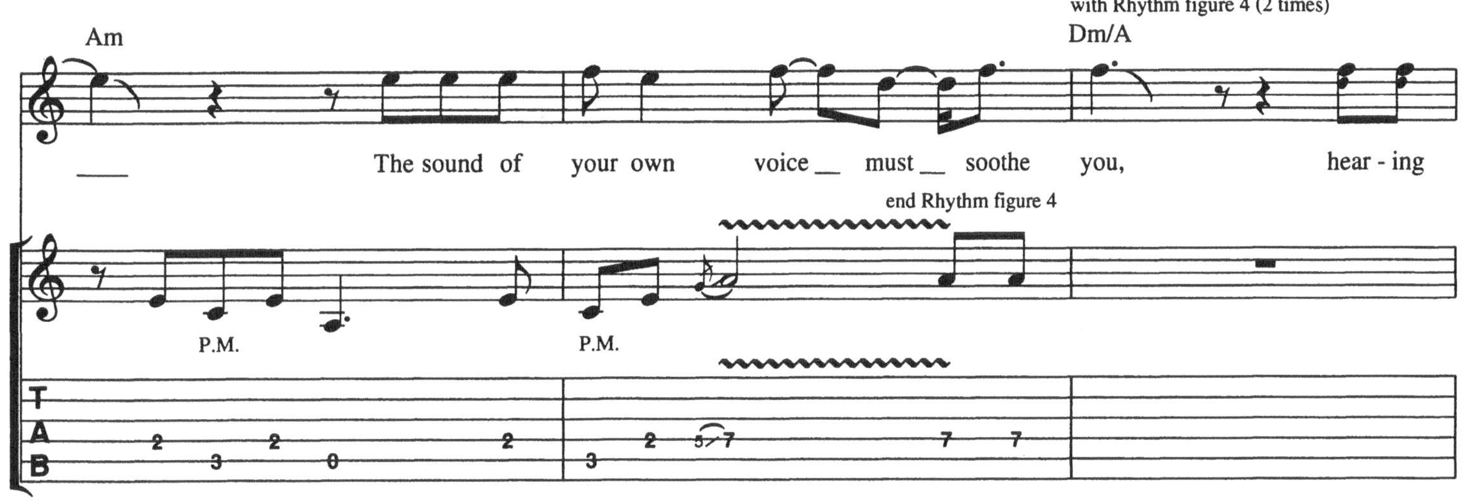

with Rhythm figure 4 (2 times)
Am
Dm/A
The sound of your own voice __ must __ soothe you, hear - ing
end Rhythm figure 4
P.M.
P.M.

Am
on - ly what you wan - na hear ______ and know-ing on - ly what you've heard. ____

Dm/A
Am
You, you're smoth-ered in trag - e - dy, _____ and you're out
guitar 3 (acoustic)
mp
let ring

A5
guitar 2
(cont. in notation)
to save __ the world. __
guitar 1
P.M.
P.M.
f
P.M.

Chorus
3rd time with Fill 2
F#5   N.C.   E5   A5   B5   F#5   N.C.   E5
Mis - er - y. ______ You in - sist that the weight of the world ____ should
guitars 1 & 2
P.M.
P.M.
P.M.
Rhythm figure 5
A5   A#5 B5 E5   F#5   N.C.   A5   B5
be on your shoul - ders. ____ Mis - er - y. ______ There's much more to life than what you see, ____
P.M.
end Rhythm figure 5   P.M.
P.M.
F#5   N.C.   E5   A5   A#5   B5 Eb6   E5   E(b6)
to Coda
my friend of mis - er - y. ______
P.M.
P.M.
P.M.
P.M.
Fill 2
guitar 6   F#5   N.C.   E5

1.
E5
Dm/A
2.
E5
Dm/A
My friend of mis - er - y.
guitar 2
guitar 1
P.M.
P.M.
P.M.
P.M.
A5
Dm/A
Interlude
Am
Dm/A
guitar 1
Am
simile (next 12 bars)
mp
* Swell with volume knob using R.H. pinky
Dm/A
Am
Dm/A
Am
(cont. in Fill 1)
B R
B R

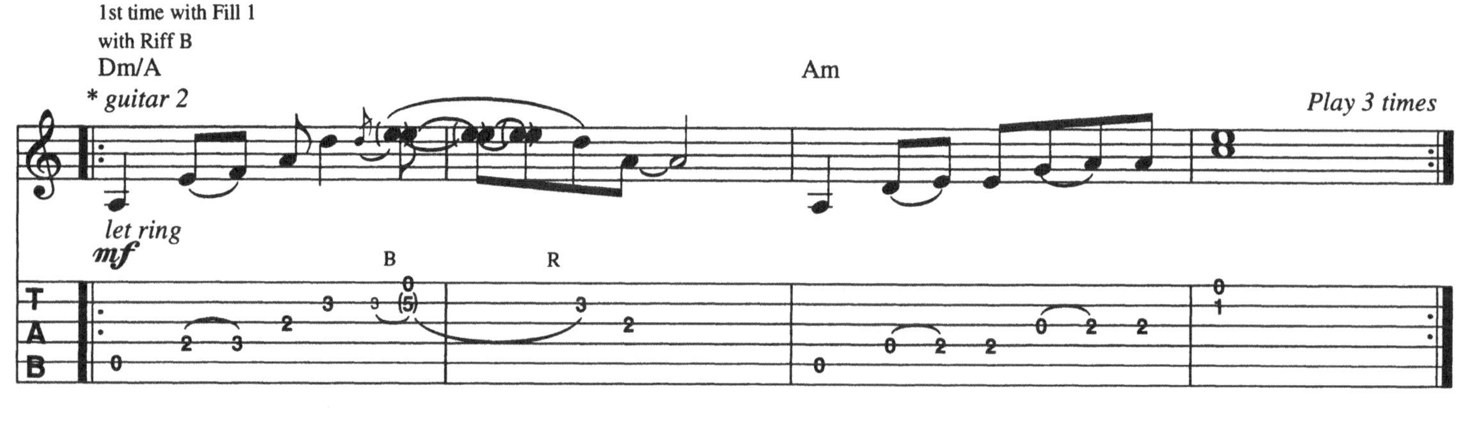

1st time with Fill 1
with Riff B
Dm/A
* guitar 2
Am
Play 3 times
let ring
mf
B
R

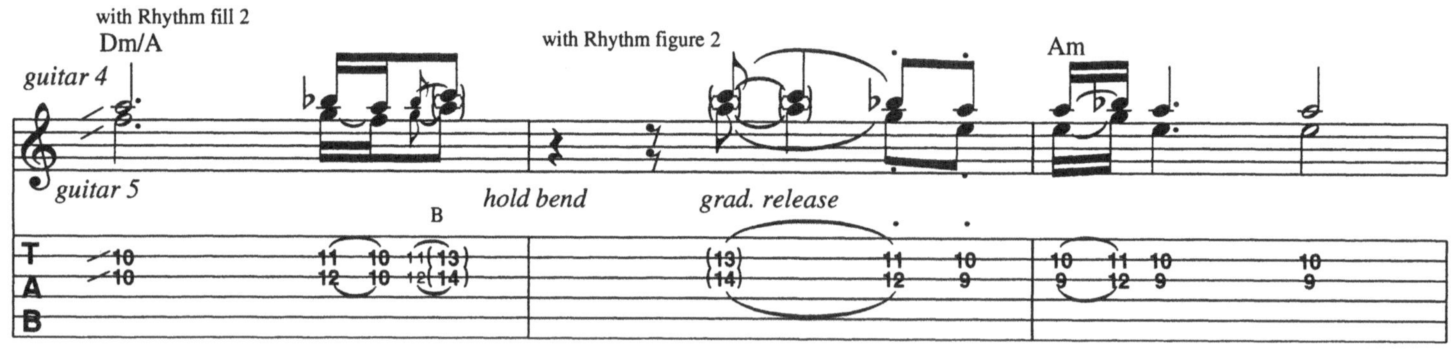

with Rhythm fill 2
Dm/A
guitar 4
with Rhythm figure 2
Am
guitar 5
hold bend
grad. release
B

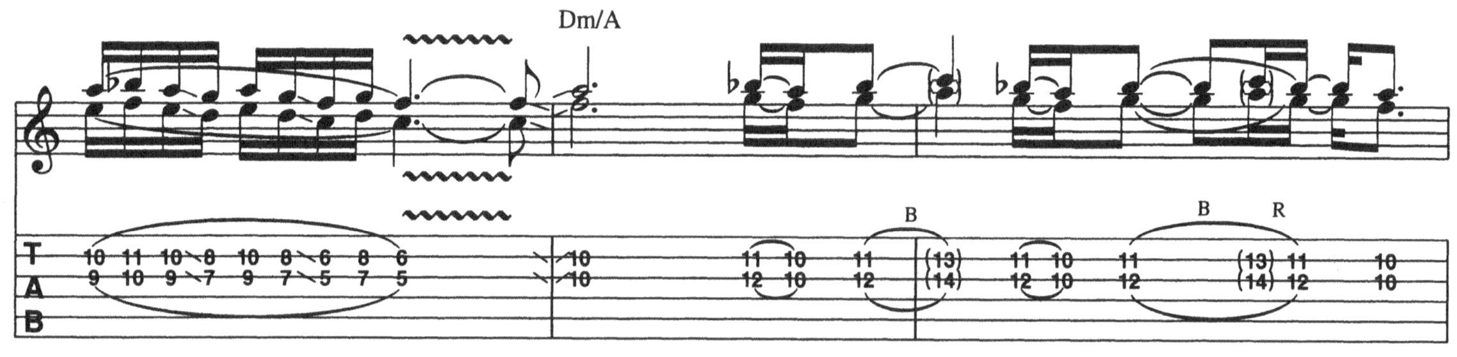

Dm/A
B
B
R

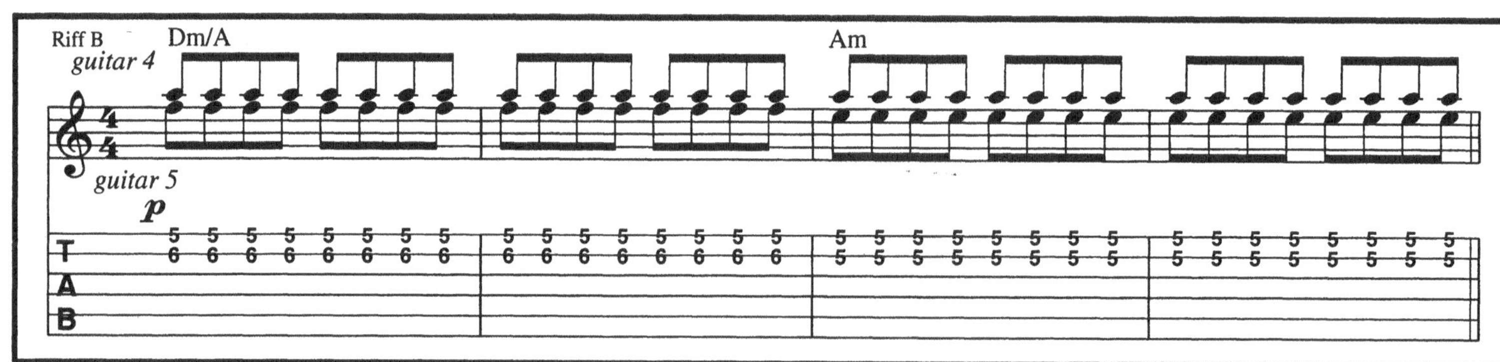

Riff B
Dm/A
guitar 4
Am
guitar 5
p

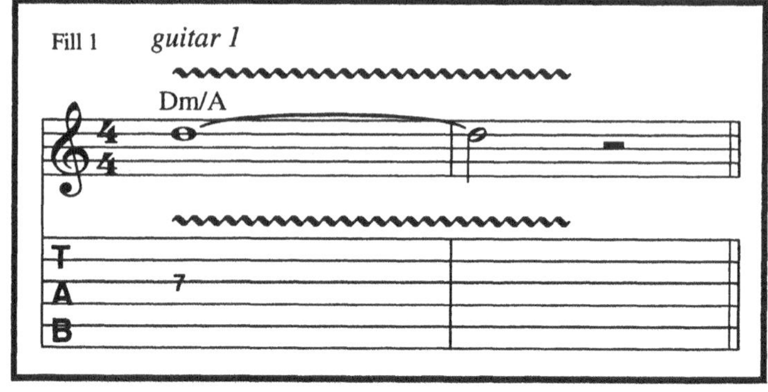

Fill 1
guitar 1
Dm/A

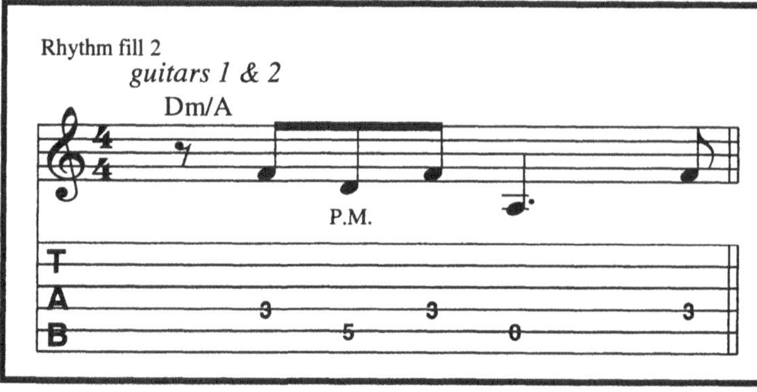

Rhythm fill 2
guitars 1 & 2
Dm/A
P.M.

with Rhythm figure 3
Dm/A

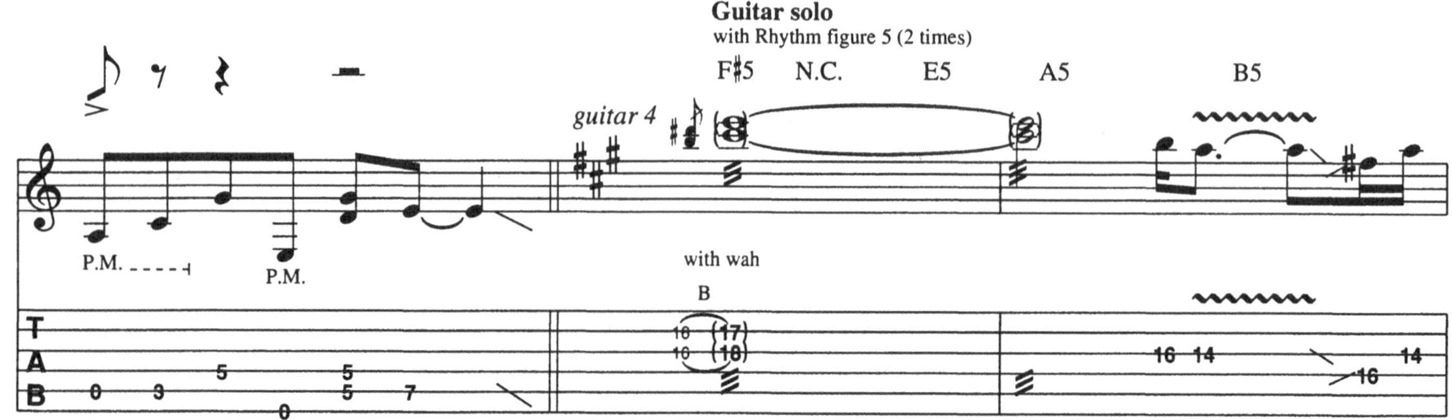

with Rhythm figure 4
Dm/A
8va
Am
A5
guitar 2
guitar 1
8va
P.M.
P.M.
B R
8va
Guitar solo
with Rhythm figure 5 (2 times)
F#5   N.C.   E5   A5   B5
guitar 4
P.M.
P.M.
with wah
B

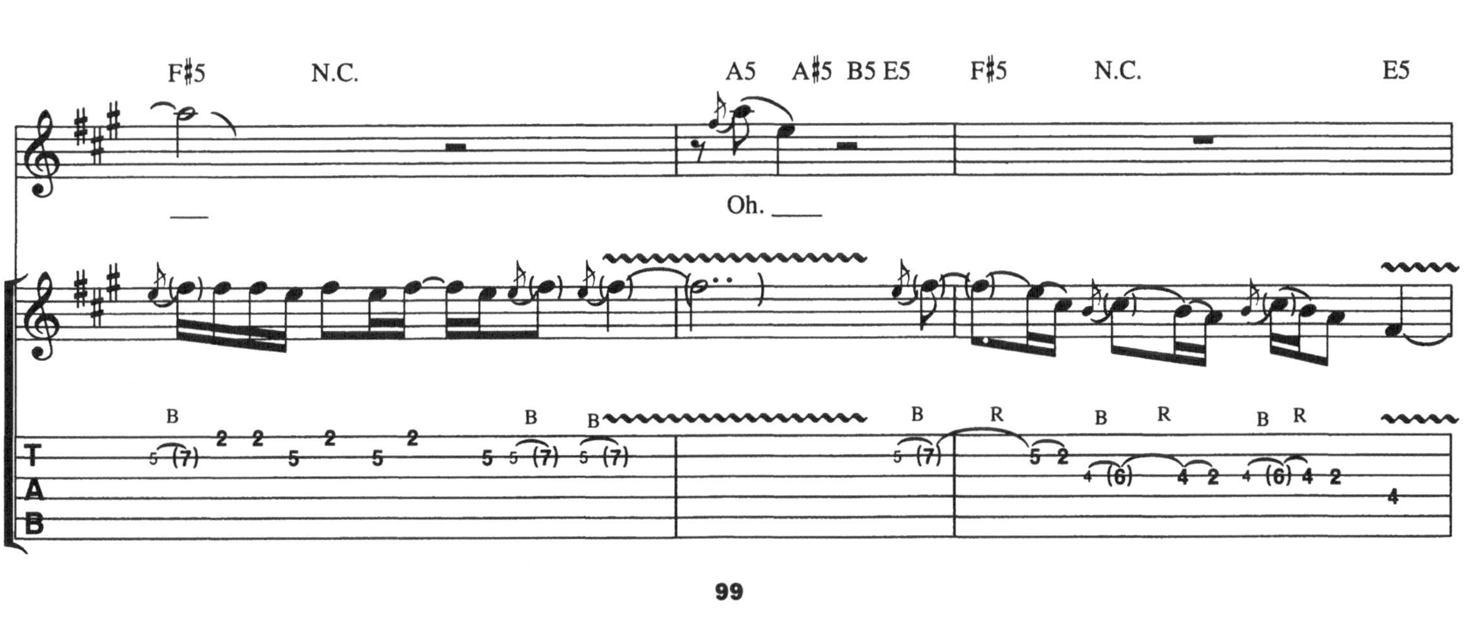

F#5 N.C. E5 A5 A#5 B5 E5 F#5 N.C. E5
8va
A5 B5 F#5 N.C. E5 A5 A#5 B5 E5
D.S. al Coda
(cont. in Fill 2)
8va
* T.B.
* Depress before striking note
Coda
Outro
w/Rhy. Fig. 5 (4 times)
E5 F#5 N.C. E5 A5 B5
You just stood there scream - ing.
(guitars 1 & 2)
guitar 6
with wah
P.M.
F#5 N.C. A5 A#5 B5 E5 F#5 N.C. E5
Oh.

My friend of mis- er - y. _______
Yeah, _______ yeah, ___ yeah!

(guitar 2)
F#5
E5 F5
F#5
6 open
E G5
Rhythm figure 6
B
hold bend
grad. release
end Rhythm figure 6
guitar 1
P.M.
with Rhythm figure 6 (3 times)
F#5
E5 F5 F#5
6 open
E G5
R
B R
B
B
B
3
3
P.M.
F#5
E5 F5
F#5
6 open
E G5
8va
3
3
7
6
3
P.M.

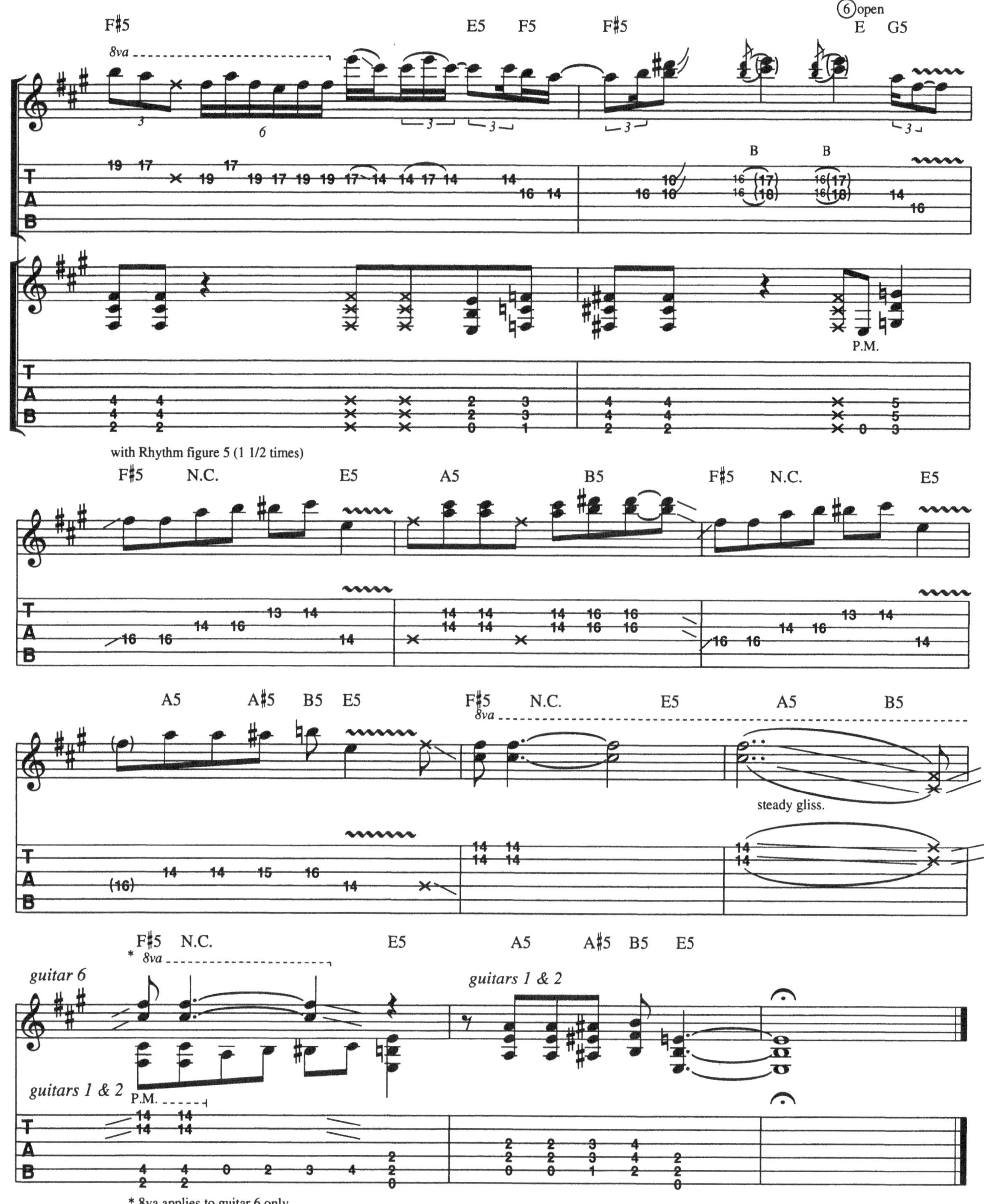

Additional lyrics

2. You still stood there screaming,
No one caring about these words you tell.
My friend, before your voice is gone,
One man's fun is another's hell.
These times are sent to try men's souls.
But something's wrong with all you see.
You, you'll take it on all yourself.
Remember, misery loves company.   *(to Chorus)*

THE STRUGGLE WITHIN

WORDS & MUSIC BY JAMES HETFIELD LARS ULRICH

103

1st Verse
E5
E5
Reach - ing out for some - thing you've got - ta feel. _____ You're clutch - ing to what you had
guitars 1 & 2
Rhy. fig. 2
G5
E5
F#5 G5
E5
P.M.
P.M.
P.M.
thought was re - al. Kick - ing at a dead horse pleas - es you. _____
F#5 G5
E5
G5
E5
F5
E5 end Rhy. fig. 2
Rhy. fig.3
F#5 G5
P.M.
P.M.
P.M.
No way of show - in' your grat - i - tude. _____ S - so man - y
F#5 G5
E5
G5
E5
G5
P.M.
P.M.
P.M.
things you don't wan - na do. _____ What is it, what have you got _____ to lose? _____
E5
F5
6 open E F5
6 open E F5
end Rhy. fig. 3
E5
F#5 G5
E5
P.M.
P.M.
P.M.
P.M.
P.M.
What the hell? _____
(What the hell?)
F#5 G5
E5
6 open E F5
6 open E F5
end Rhy. fig. 4
E5
G5
P.M.
P.M.
What is it you think you're gon - na find? _____ Hyp - o - crite.
(Hyp - o - crite.)
E5
G5
E5
G5
6 open E G5
6 open E G5
P.M.
P.M.
P.M.
P.M.
Bore - dom sets in - to the bor - ing mind. _____

Half time feel
guitar 1
G5   F5   G5   F5
P.M.   Rhythm figure 5A
P.M.
P.M.
P.M.
end Rhythm figure 5A
guitar 2
P.M.   Rhythm figure 5B
P.M.
P.M.
P.M.
end Rhythm figure 5B
Chorus
Rhythm figure 6
F#5   E5   F#5   E5
with Rhythm figure 6 (3 times)
guitars 1 & 2
end Rhythm figure 6
It suits you fine. _
(Strug - gle with - in.) __
Your ru - in.
(Strug - gle with - in.) __
F#5   E5   F#5   E5
You seal _ your own _ cof - fin. ____
(Strug - gle with - in.) _
The strug - gl - ing _ with - in. _
(Strug - gle with - in.) _
with Rhythm figure 5B
G5   F5   G5   F5
guitar 1
P.M.   Rhythm figure 5C
P.M.
P.M.
P.M.
end Rhythm figure 5C

with Fill 2
E5
(end half time feel)
P.M.
rit.
Feedback
2/4

with Rhythm figure 1 (2 1/2 times)
2/4
a tempo
*
* Let feedback ring as chord decays

2nd Verse
with Rhythm figure 2
E5   G5   E5   F#5 G5 E5
substitute Rhy. fill 1   resume Rhy. fig. 2
F#5   E5
Home is not a home, it   be - comes a hell. _________   Turn - ing   it   in - to   a

with Rhy. fig. 3 (1st 9 bars only)
G5   E5   F5   E5   F#5 G5 E5   F#5 G5
pris - on cell. _________   Ad - van - tag - es are tak - en,   not   hand - ed   out. ___

Fill 2   E5
guitar 2
rake
4/4

Rhy. fill 1   guitars 1 & 2   F#5
2/4
P.M. - - - - - - - - - -

While you strug - gle in - side your hell,
ow.
(Reach - ing out.)
Reach- ing out.
Grab - bing for
some - thing you've got to feel.
Clos - ing in.
The
pres - sure up - on you is so un - real.
Half time feel
with Rhythm figures 5A & 5B
Chorus
with Rhythm figure 6
It suits you fine.
Your ru - in.
(Strug - gle with - in.)
(Strug - gle with - in.)
You seal your own cof - fin.
S - strug -gl - ing with - in
(Strug - gle with - in.)
(Strug - gle with - in.)
with Rhythm figures 5B & 5C

with Fill 3
E5
guitar 1
(end half time feel)
P.M.
rit.
Feedback
(Vocal:) Struggle.
a tempo
Guitar solo
Rhy. fig. 7
guitars 1 & 2
E5
G5
E5
G5
end Rhy. fig. 7
with Rhythm figure 7 (3 times)
E5
G5
P.M.
E5
G5
E5
G5
E5
G5
8va
B R B
E5
G5
E5
G5
G5
Bb5
Rhy. fig. 8
P.M.
8va
Fill 3
E5
guitar 2
(15ma)
rake
a tempo
Feedback
P.M.

G5
Bb5
end Rhy. fig. 8
with Rhythm figure 8 (3 times)
G5
Bb5
G5
Bb5
P.M.
8va
G5
Bb5
G5
Bb5
G5
(15ma)
Bb5
8va
B hold bend
A.H.
Half time feel
with Rhythm figure 6 (4 times)
G5
(15ma)
Bb5
F#5
E5
P.M.
A.H.
with wah
F#5
E5
F#5
B
B
E5
F#5
E5
vib. lower note only
B
B
R B
B

with Rhythm figure 8
G5
Bb5
G5
Bb5
G5
Ab5 Bb5
P.M.
8va
3
3
3
3
3
3
3
3

G5
Ab5
6 open
E Ab5
6 open
E Ab5
Ab5
6 open
E Ab5
6 open
E Ab5
P.M.
P.M.
P.M.
P.M.
P.M.
8va
3/4
with wah effects
wah off
B
U.B.
4/4

G5
(8va)
E5 G5 E5
E5 G5 E5
guitars
1 & 2
(Vocal:) Go!
A.H.
B
P.M.
P.M.

E5 G5 E5
A5 Ab5 G5
Gb5 F5
F5
P.M.
P.M.
2/4

3rd Verse
with Rhythm figure 3
E5 F#5 G5 E5
F#5 G5 E5
G5
2/4
Reach - ing out for some - thing you've got to feel._______ While clutch - ing to

with Rhythm figure 4 (2 times)
E5
G5 E5
F5
E5
3/4
2/4
what you had thought was real.___________ What the hell?____

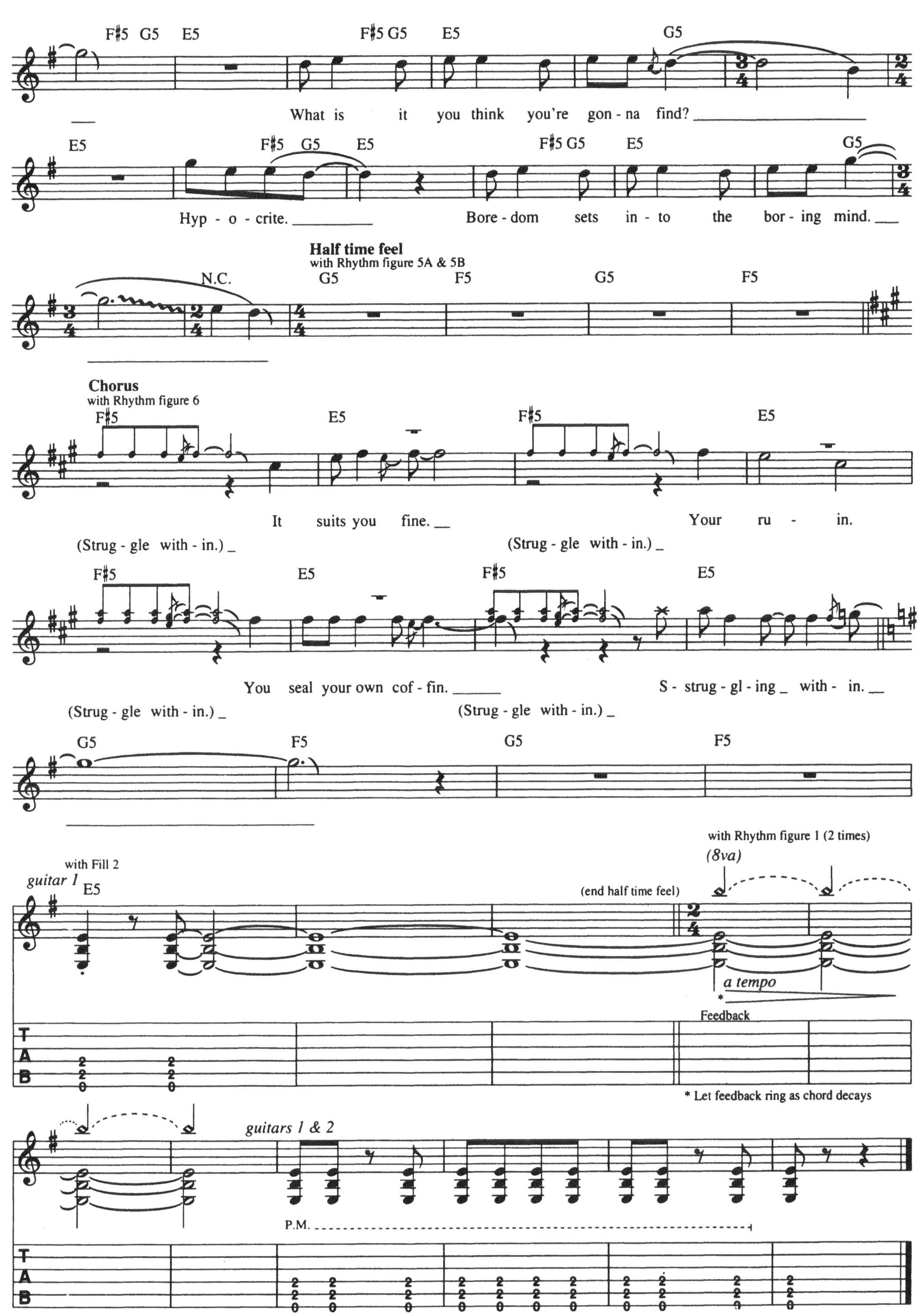

F#5 G5 E5
F#5 G5 E5
G5
What is it you think you're gon - na find?
E5
F#5 G5 E5
F#5 G5 E5
G5
Hyp - o - crite.
Bore - dom sets in - to the bor - ing mind.
Half time feel
with Rhythm figure 5A & 5B
N.C.
G5
F5
G5
F5
Chorus
with Rhythm figure 6
F#5
E5
F#5
E5
It suits you fine.
Your ru - in.
(Strug - gle with - in.)
(Strug - gle with - in.)
F#5
E5
F#5
E5
You seal your own cof - fin.
S - strug - gl - ing with - in.
(Strug - gle with - in.)
(Strug - gle with - in.)
G5
F5
G5
F5
with Fill 2
guitar 1
E5
with Rhythm figure 1 (2 times)
(8va)
(end half time feel)
a tempo
Feedback
* Let feedback ring as chord decays
guitars 1 & 2
P.M.

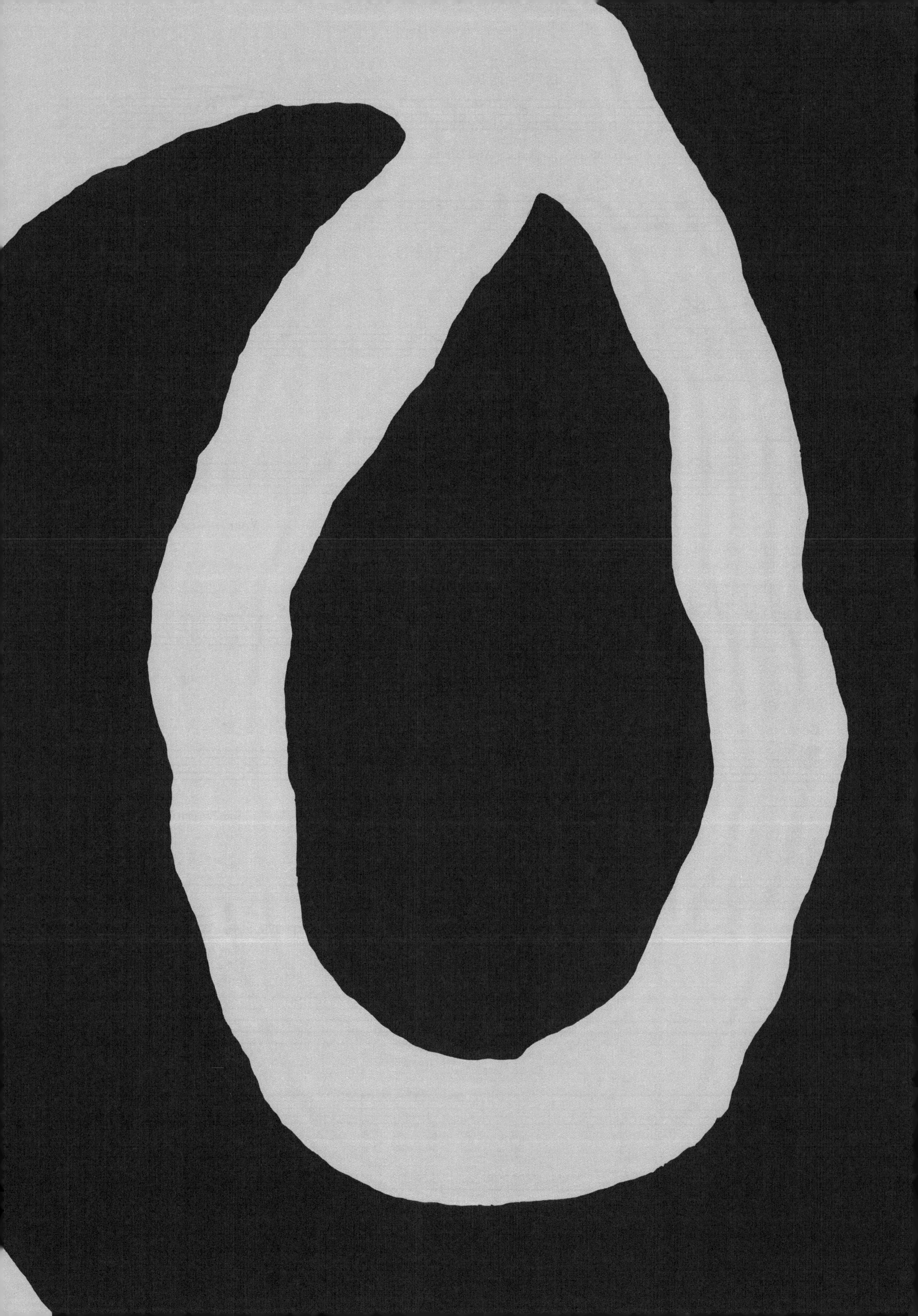